ART IN
CRAFTMAKING

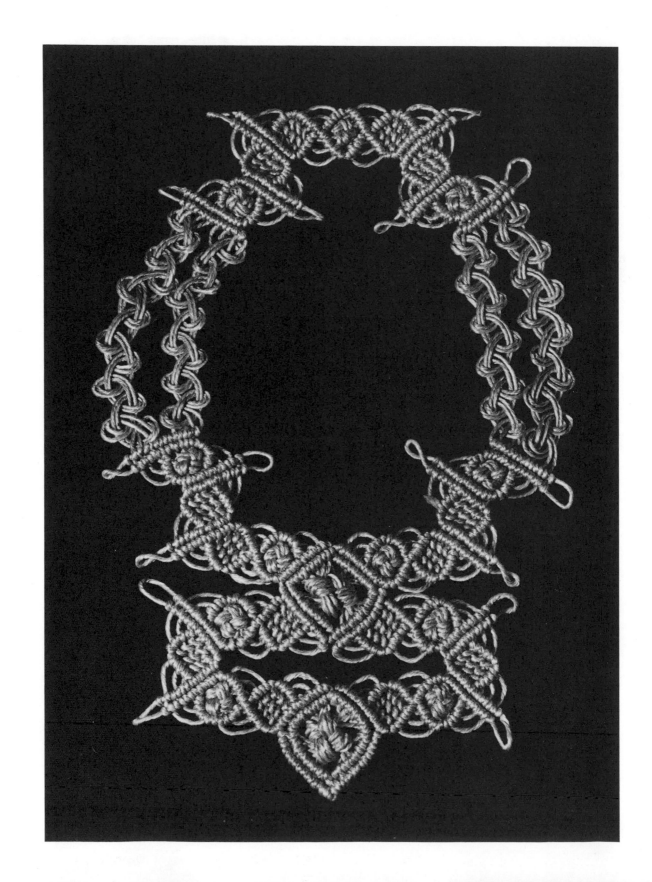

ART IN CRAFTMAKING

Basic Methods and Materials

Carolyn S. Howlett

VNR VAN NOSTRAND REINHOLD COMPANY
NEW YORK   CINCINNATI   TORONTO   LONDON   MELBOURNE
   1974   176 pg.

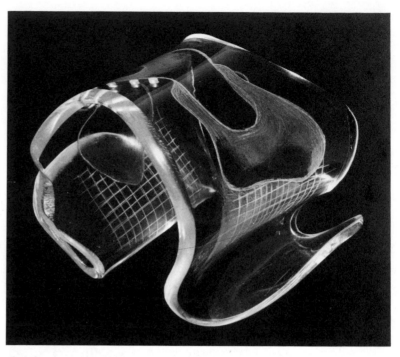

Van Nostrand Reinhold Company Regional Offices:
New York Cincinnati Chicago Millbrae Dallas

Van Nostrand Reinhold Company International Offices:
London Toronto Melbourne

Designed by Elaine M. Gongora
Photographs by James W. Howlett, unless otherwise credited.

Diagrams by the author, except those on page 156,
by Joan Paque.

Published by Van Nostrand Reinhold Company
450 West 33rd Street, New York, N.Y. 10001

Published simultaneously in Canada by
Van Nostrand Reinhold Limited

16 15 14 13 12 11 10 9 8 7 6 5 4 3 2 1

Library of Congress Cataloging in Publication Data
Howlett, Carolyn (Svrluga) 1914-
    Art in craftmaking.
    Bibliography: p.
    1. Handicraft. I. Title.
TT145.H77   745.5   78-181442
ISBN 0-442-23559-3

Identification of works not accompanied by captions:
Half-title page: Wood experiments converted to candle-
holders by Charles Kaplan. *Frontispiece:* Macramé necklace
by Joan Paque. *Title page:* Example of surface treatment;
burning related to edge cutting and wood grain. *Copy-
right page:* Plastic bracelet. *Acknowledgments page:* Horse
marionette; polychrome wood with metal overlays and
fiber details. (Collection: Elizabeth Stein.) *Part I opener:*
Pedestal view of pendant by Michael Banner. *Part II
opener:* Toy scuba diver; hardware castaways joined with
wire and epoxy cement. (Courtesy: Syosset High School,
New York.) *Part III opener:* Silver pin by Michael Jerry.
Part IV opener: Bowls by three craftsmen. Upper row:
James Prestini, 1939 and 1940. Center: Reynold G. Dennis,
1951. Below: Tapie Wirkkala, 1951. (Collection: The
Museum of Modern Art, New York.)

Acknowledgments

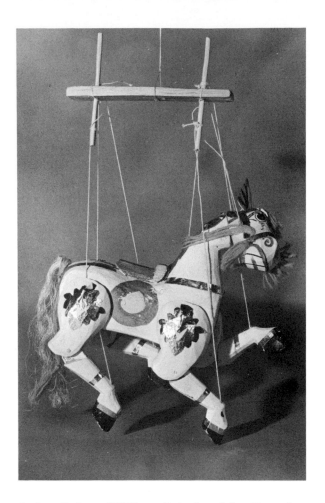

This book is an outgrowth of the content of my courses in crafts and design as taught at the School of the Art Institute of Chicago. The continuing interest and requests for new material from my many former students, who are now teaching throughout the country, inspired and encouraged the preparation of this volume.

Among the Art Institute graduates who contributed illustrative examples are: Lloyd New, Director of the Institute of American Indian Arts; Lynn de Rosa, teacher of Art and Humanities in Syosset, New York; and Elizabeth Stein, whose private collection of materials and objects of good design provided an invaluable asset.

I extend special thanks to the following people for their assistance in the procurement of photographs of works by professional artists and craftsmen: Dr. Eleanor Caldwell, Chairman of Invitational Crafts Exhibitions at the Oakbrook Center in Illinois; Ellen Marsh of the Museum of Modern Art in New York; Ronald Stokes, Director of Education at the Milwaukee Art Center; and Madeleine Tourtelot, Director of the Peninsula School of Arts in Door County, Wisconsin.

The excellent examples by students of the Chicago Public Schools were made available through the efforts and cooperation of Mary Cole Emerson, Director of Art.

The preliminary reading and response to the manuscript in progress by Herbert Bassman, and the adaptive cooperation of Elaine Montgomery in typing and retyping of the manuscript kept the work on the move.

It is virtually impossible to find the right words to thank someone so near as a "husband-photographer," who lived and worked with the total project from its very inception. Unless otherwise credited, all of the photographs in the book are the work of James W. Howlett.

I am especially grateful to all those on the staff of Van Nostrand Reinhold who assisted in the preparation of the book: to Jean Koefoed for his patient guidance in the selection of content; and to Dori Watson Boynton for her skill and understanding in the final editing of the manuscript and correlation of text with illustrations.

Above all, I appreciate the creative talents of my students at the School of the Art Institute. I only regret that all of their names are not identified as some of their work was photographed candidly at informal school exhibits. I am pleased and proud to acknowledge the names of the following individuals who conceived and made many of the examples shown: Helen Berge, Emile Bergeron, Allan Berman, Arthur Bolton, William Brincka, John Brumley, Vita Cernius, Anthony Chelz, Geraldine Ciffone, Jeannreine Cole, Don Cortese, Dorothy de Wall, Robert Dominiak, John Doyle, Mary Frank, Roger Garfield, Nancy Barsamian, John Jefchak, Arlene Kukielka, Susan Lorimer, Gerald Moeller, Roberta Berg, Maureen Capraro, Nelson Dodson, Jolynn Doerr, Carl Hayano, Jay Hinz, Richard Hunt, Richard M. Johnson, Sharon Kouris, Joyce Michalski, Pamela Share Nisson, Nan Orvis, Barbara Pechtel, James Peterson, Kathleen Pietrucha, Margaret Powell, Jackie Pressler, Marcia Reidel, Irene Salava, Jasper San Fratello, Robert Savlin, Richard Scott, Ann Burnham Smith, Bernard Solomon, Linda Stephens, Donna Sved, Lorraine Ellen Straw, Helen Van Dyke Tempera, Otto Thieme, Charles Thompson, Dick Westgard, Richard Watson, Susan Wiese, Mary Wisnieski, Georgia Wulff, Ron Ysla, and Joseph Zeller.

A large measure of thanks is due to those graduates who worked so diligently as assistants in the materials workshops: Charles Alberti, Penny Jackson, Barbara Erickson Highland, Ida Horowitz, Stephen Husarik, Jr., Katherine A. Jelinek, Frances Kokotis, Karen Mong, Jane Redmond, Earl Teteak, Rene Michele-Trapaga, and Betty Williams.

Finally, I wish to commend those members of the faculty who served as assistant instructors: Ann Ceithaml, John Cook, Rosemary Demkovich, Julie Greenis, Leonard Mickas, Marjorie Price, and Frances Ronvik.

Contents

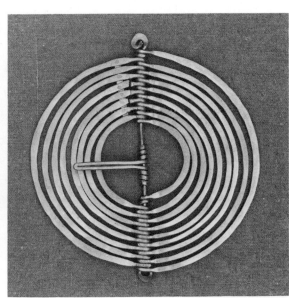

8

PART ONE
LOOKING AT CRAFTS

The concrete jungle.

Supermarket sameness.

Crafts of anonymity.

CHAPTER 1/Introduction to Crafts

Crafts and the Need for Individuality

The need for individuality is widely recognized as a major challenge of the technological age. In a world dominated by the speed and efficiency of mass production, the environment has become increasingly more standardized and impersonal. With each new development in push-button living, man has been subjected to new forces of conformity. Although he enjoys the assets of the "good life" with a bountiful supply of mass-produced things, he is becoming more and more aware of the liabilities of anonymity as a way of life. He is searching for ways to self-identification.

The individual on his own can do little about the maze of concrete jungles that engulf him. Large-scale structures of sameness are uncompromisingly set. They stand aloof in their bigness.

The monotonous uniformity of prefabrication also pervades the immediate home environment. The stark, boxlike shapes of major appliances have become an indispensable part of every household. Only the labels and slight differences in the shapes of handles and knobs distinguish one make of stove, refrigerator and washer from another. These are the kinds of products that epitomize functional efficiency but defy even the most minimal changes a person may want to make in their design or appearance.

Craft objects, however, are of much smaller scale and relate to the response of the individual as a person. They are the kinds of things he can hold, touch, and fondle. They are the things he enjoys wearing, like belts, sandals and jewelry; or needs and wants for his home, like bowls, boxes and trays; or likes to have for fun and play, like games, puzzles and toys. While quantities of craft objects are mass-produced and easy to get anywhere, the individual is no longer satisfied with things that are available by the dozen. He searches through piles of identical items in department stores and gift shops for that "something different" that will give him a chance to be himself in some uniquely special way.

The making of craft objects offers a way to satisfy this desire for things that are different. It is a way for an individual to become directly involved in personalizing his own environment. It is a way for him to experience the pleasure and satisfaction of fulfillment that come with the creative conception and evolution of the form of an object from beginning to end. Since this is the way of art, it is important to consider the methods and means of the artist as they relate to those of the craftsman. This is the purpose of looking at crafts from a fine-arts point of view.

Running Horse Weathervane. Sheet iron, American, 18th Century. (Courtesy: The Art Institute of Chicago.)

Crafts from a Fine-Arts View

In looking at crafts from a fine-arts view, the useful object is recognized as a vehicle for the personal expression of the individual. The new trends in contemporary painting and sculpture as well as in the crafts have done much to foster this kind of recognition. In fact, they reveal that the artist and craftsman have already joined forces in their common search for individuality.

MERGERS IN MATERIALS AND PROCESSES

One of the most influential trends in all forms of visual art is characterized by mergers in the use of materials and processes. The new look of painting and sculpture today has more linkage with the crafts than with the traditional framed canvases and sculptures set up on pedestals.

More and more, contemporary painters, abandoning stretched canvases and easel painting, have been bypassing the conventional art supply stores in favor of the craftsman's usual supply sources: lumberyards, hardware stores, junk yards and electronic centers. Pipes, nuts and bolts as well as plywood and house paint have become the artist's new "palette." The materials and processes that were generally considered the domain of the craftsman have been taken over and become the artistic vocabulary for the painter and sculptor. The Pop-Art artist, for example, has transgressed all the barriers between the arts through his dramatic transformations of useful objects and products of the everyday world into works of art. He is more inclined to sew and stuff fabric or model in papier-mâché than to paint on canvas or carve a block of marble. There are numerous other examples in museum collections of shaped canvases and structural paintings that are typical of the ways that craft materials and processes have become part of the mainstream of the fine arts.

America-Dawn by Louise Nevelson, 1962–1967. Wood, painted white; 216" x 168" x 120". (Courtesy: The Art Institute of Chicago.)

Dormeyer Mixer by Claes Oldenburg. Vinyl, wood and kapok. (Collection: Whitney Museum of American Art. Gift of the Howard and Jean Lipman Foundation.)

(Above) Brooch by Michael Jerry. Cast silver.

(Left) *Family* by Marisol. (Collection: Mr. and Mrs. Robert B. Mayer.)

ACTION AND MOTION

The emphasis on action and motion is another significant trend in the arts that is especially relevant to the crafts. Many of the methods and techniques that are now being used by the artist to express movement have had their heritage in the crafts. Moving parts and multisensory stimuli have long been a "natural" in the design and construction of crafts for ceremonial pageantry and adornment. The masks, puppets, dolls, kites and games that were made by peoples and cultures throughout the ages are typical forerunners of kinetic art concepts.

Shadow puppet of Lion Dog. North China, 19th Century. (Courtesy: The Field Museum of Natural History, Chicago.)

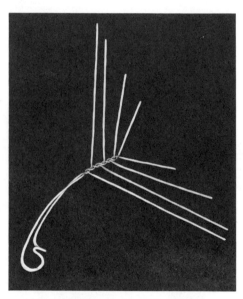

Brooch by Alexander Calder, 1930's or 40's. Hammered silver; 12⅜" x 9½" x 5/16". (Collection: The Museum of Modern Art, New York. Gift of the Artist.)

Peg Bus. Natural wood and orange lacquer finish. (Courtesy: Creative Playthings, Inc.)

Puzzle Sculpture by Edward Mayer. Redwood; 6" x 6" x 38". (Collection: Milwaukee Art Center.)

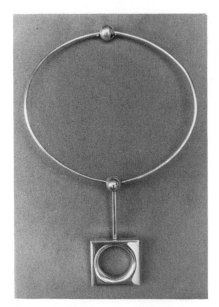

Geometric Necklace by Michael Jerry.

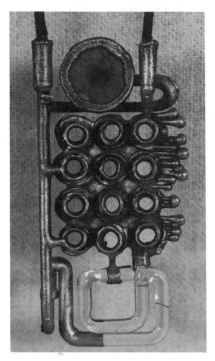

Electroformed Pendant by Lee B. Peck, 1969. Silver-plated copper with plastic inlay and glass rod.

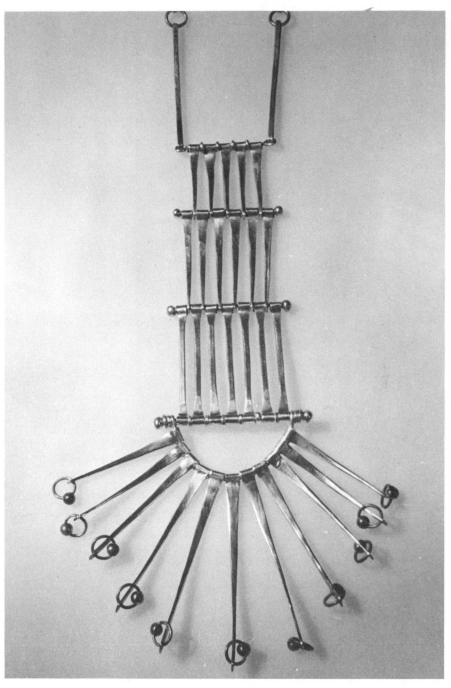

Mobile Necklace by Tone Vigeland, Norway. (Collection: Ellen Kluck.)

ARTIST AS CRAFTSMAN

The contemporary artist who is concerned with the participative involvement of the viewer often turns to craftmaking. He finds that the design and structure of sculptural puzzles, playing blocks and other movable toys and games provide intriguing incentives for his work. He also finds that jewelry-making offers a great many possibilities for the creation of multifaceted images. Necklaces, bracelets, earrings, anklets and other types of body jewelry are stirred to sound and motion by the human figure that wears them; together, they create the changes in image that are so expressive of contemporary life and living.

The work of the artist as craftsman has given a new kind of

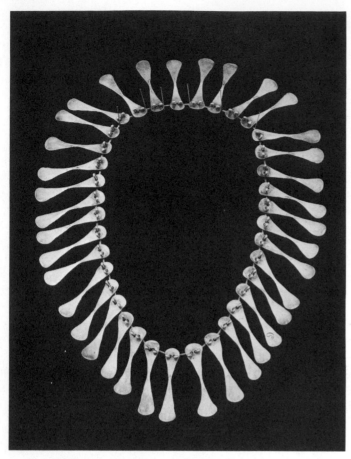

Brooch by Mary Walker.

Necklace by Harun Abdulrashid. Silver wire with soldered terminals.

Necklace by Alexander Calder, 1941. Hammered silver; inner circumference 26", outer circumference 43". (Collection: The Museum of Modern Art, New York. James Thrall Soby Fund.)

Kachina Face by James Honyaktewa. Hopi. Brooch of silver with inlays of bone, turquoise, coral and wood. (Courtesy: Institute of American Indian Arts, Sante Fe, New Mexico. Photo: Kay Wiest.)

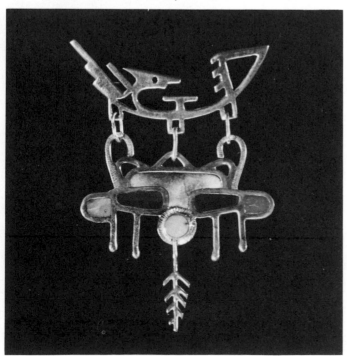

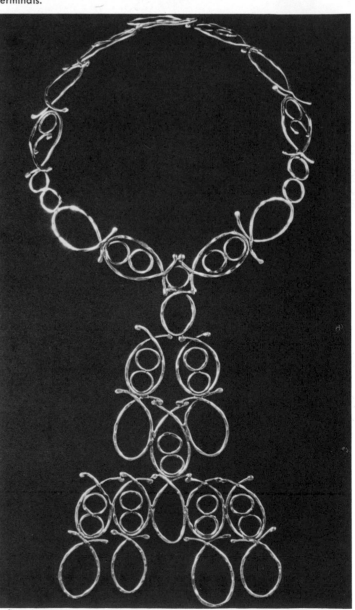

Piggy #1 by Valenza, 1966. Walnut jewelry box. (Photo: U.N.H.)

status to the self-expressive role of the useful craft object. His jewelry, bowls, tableware, boxes and toys have proved to be just as revealing of his meaning and purpose as any of his non-utilitarian work.

CRAFTSMAN AS ARTIST

The professional craftsman has reciprocated for the invasion of his "territory" by the artist and sculptor. He has transformed the craft object into a highly individual form of expression. His work reflects the same freedom in the use of materials, the same adventurous experimentation, and the same unpredictable outcomes that characterize creative production in painting and sculpture.

It should be remembered that the reasons for craftmaking today are very different from the days when necessity prompted the making of these objects. In a world where mass-made products are so readily and cheaply available, the crafts have been released from bondage to mere utility. The functional aspect of the craft object has a vital new role in the creative process; it serves as the spark that ignites the conception of ideas for personal expression. Even the "finest" of fine-arts artists sets up limitations for himself as a point of departure for his work. The usability of an object provides a similar incentive for the craftsman.

The following statement by Bernard Roberts reflects the new attitudes and purposes that pervade the work of the craftsman as

17

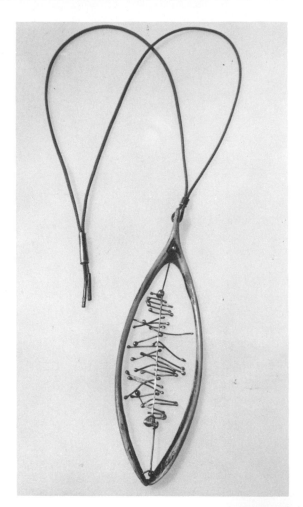

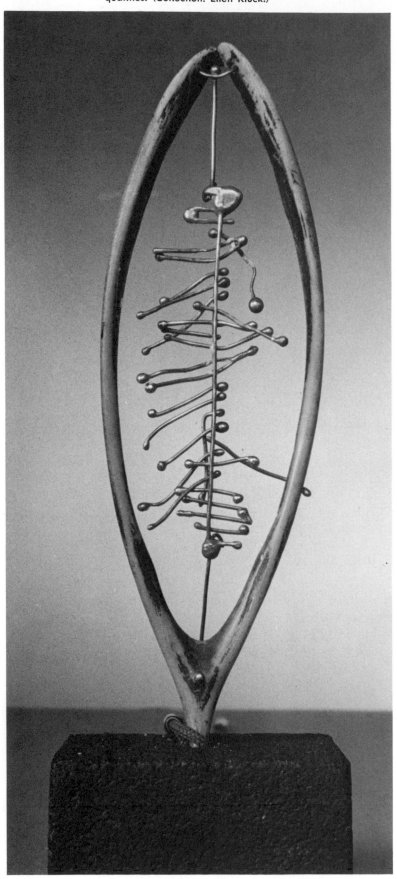

Pendant by Michael Banner. Wood and cast metal. This pendant is shown on a pedestal on page 8. (Collection: Ellen Kluck.)

Myrtlewood bowl by Valenza. 17″ long. (Photo: U.N.H.)

artist. "I view my bowls as sculpture forms with a utilitarian function . . . they 'work' better than a more purposeful container in that they enhance the objects they contain. My fruit bowls look very fruitful when they are used."

Just as the contemporary sculptor has taken his work "off the pedestal" to convey new aims and purposes, so it is possible for the craftsman to reverse the procedure to arouse a new awareness and appreciation for the art quality of his work. Some of the examples included here show that the sculptural qualities of bowls and jewelry can be revealed more emphatically by taking them out of their usual context and displaying them from a different viewpoint, one that is generally associated with works of sculpture on a pedestal.

A comparison of the work by the different artists and craftsmen shows the diversity of ways that they have adapted the same kinds of materials into crafts for similar purposes. They show a range of opposites in response to the material and function as well as in technique and style: from the boldest, most vigorous and casually crude to the most subtle, sensitive and precisely refined. They are all examples of the personally expressive forms that relate the crafts to art.

The Materials Approach

The creative artist does not rely on a prescribed pattern but experiments freely with his materials and techniques. So, too, the craftsman who aims for individuality in his work should not be content to merely duplicate or copy a craft pattern that has been worked out by someone else. He needs to approach his work in a new way, one which will allow him the same degree of flexibility the artist has in using materials to express his own ideas. The materials approach to craftmaking described here fulfills this need.

In this approach, the material itself serves as a starting point for inquiry and action. The materials are first thoroughly explored by experimentally cutting, fastening, and manipulating them with appropriate tools. The experimental results can then be converted di-

19

Head and shoulder mask. Raffia and rope. The contour was pre-planned in quick sketches after experimentation with the manipulative possibilities of the material. The rope was shaped and fastened by sewing through it with heavy button thread.

Two views of a sculptural bowl by Bernard Roberts.

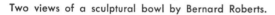

Paper sculpture. The structure was created out of a single piece of paper.

rectly into a functional craft object, or the knowledge thus gained can be applied when planning a craft object to suit a predetermined need.

This approach differs greatly from one in which a prescribed pattern for structuring the material is followed. While the latter method does eliminate many of the hazards of chance inherent in experimentation, it also excludes the kind of excitement that comes with the inventive discovery of new forms and new structural possibilities. The active investigation of each material provides the basis for craft designs that are both functional and personally expressive. This is because each person's interests, attitudes and curiosity about the same kind of material differ markedly from another person's, and the response to the material will vary. Regardless of what kind of material is used—new or salvaged, cheap or costly, rare or common— the results of each person's experimentation with it will be unique.

Since each material does have its own special qualities and characteristics, experimentation will reveal that some cutting, fastening and manipulatory processes are more suitable to one material than to another. But trial and error will also reveal more possibilities than could ever be discovered by merely following someone else's instructions for putting together pieces of a pattern. The contents of this book will show the variety of design achieved by using the materials approach to craftmaking, whether it is applied to craft objects relying on the assemblage of ready-shaped materials or to craft objects which are completely structured from raw materials.

Assemblage is a quick and easy way of making craft objects. It consists of putting together readily available materials (seashells, safety pins, etc.) that have desirable shapes and forms. This requires a minimal knowledge of cutting, fastening and manipulatory processes. In order to structure raw materials, however, more attention must be given both to the nature of the material and to the processes involved in shaping it. These two things are closely interrelated. An examination of commonly used craft materials will show that appropriate shaping or structuring processes will depend on whether the material is primarily flexible, rigid or linear.

An entire section of the book, therefore, deals with the exploration of materials in terms of these three categories and with the experimentation with structuring processes related to those categories. The categories, of course, are not absolute. A thin sheet of cork may be classified as flexible and lend itself to manipulation such as folding, while a thick block of the same material may exhibit more rigid characteristics and lend itself more readily to subtractive shaping through carving. A number of passages, therefore, deal with each individual material in terms of the variety of forms it may take and its special characteristics.

Finally, when exploration and experimentation have been completed, the results can be adapted into a craft object through three different methods of design: experimental, preplanned or spontaneous. These methods are explained in Chapter 6.

The materials approach to craftmaking will enrich not only the design quality of the finished object, but the personal rewards of making it as well.

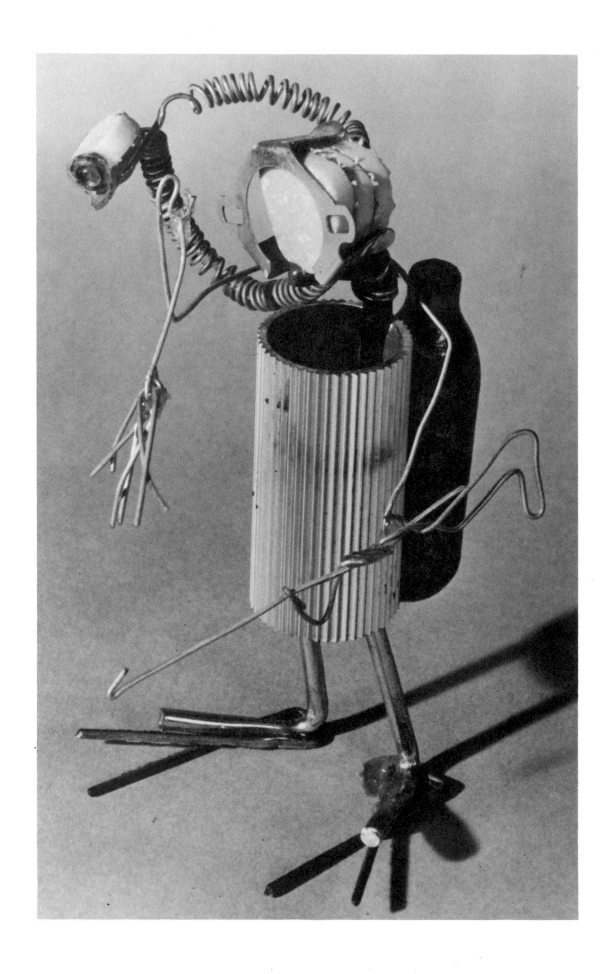

PART TWO
CRAFTS OF ASSEMBLAGE

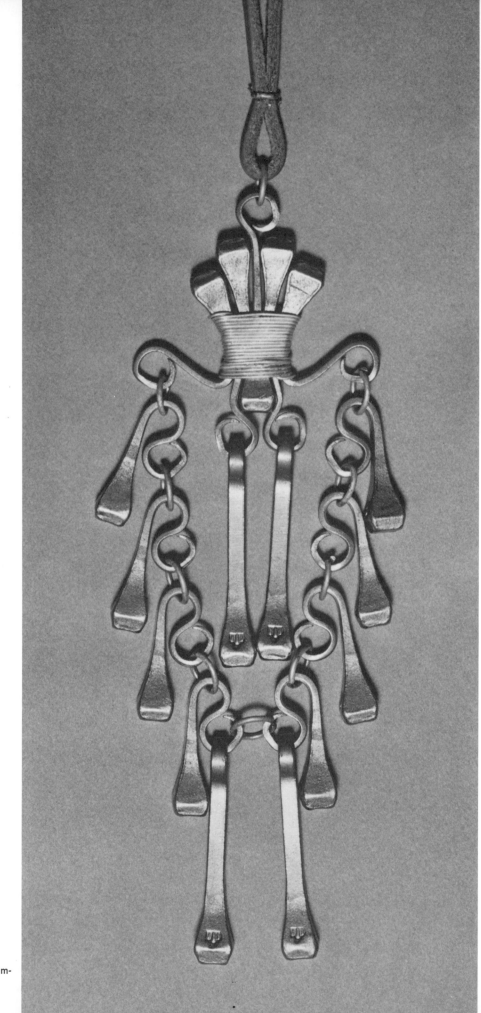

Necklace of horseshoe nails. Contemporary Italian.

CHAPTER 2/Assemblage: Definition and Processes

Assemblage is one of the most effective ways to develop individuality of expression in craftmaking. The results can be achieved quickly and provide immediate satisfaction of accomplishment. The process is primarily concerned with the putting together of castaway materials and commonplace items. Little or no preplanning of designs is needed or even desirable. The conception of ideas for things to make and how to make them evolves through working directly with the material. The process involves three basic steps:

1. The finding and selection of interesting material.
2. The arrangement and grouping of the material to develop ideas for useful craft possibilities.
3. The joining, fastening and finishing of the material to make it functional for a chosen purpose.

Each of these steps offers numerous opportunities for personal expression. The type of material selected is a revealing clue to a person's interests and attitudes as well as his perceptual awareness. Much of the look and spirit of the final craft object is determined by what materials were found and chosen in the first place.

As a person collects the material, he learns how to see and enjoy its special qualities and is simultaneously motivated to do things with it and to make something from it. The existing sizes and shapes of the pieces and parts provide something tangible to touch, handle, push and move around. They invite the kind of carefree and playful arrangements and rearrangements that suggest various craft possibilities. These, in turn, call for the exploration of methods of attachment and finishing that are suitable for the particular materials and craft purpose. It is largely through this final step of the process that the individual develops his ingenuity in solving practical problems in inventive and imaginative ways.

The next three chapters deal with the assemblage of crafts from three different sources of material: nature's castaways; man-made castaways; and ready-mades. Each chapter defines the unique qualities and advantages of the particular type of material and shows examples of the diversity of ways that different individuals have used it for creative craftmaking.

The remainder of this chapter describes the various methods for joining the elements of an assemblage. Joining is divided into two kinds: detachable and permanent. The joining method used will depend upon the sort of object being made and the materials involved.

Cigarette Server. Experimental design in wood converted
to a functional purpose. Holes and wedging were used to
create an additive structure.

Candleholder made of clothespins.

Joining and Fastening Methods: Detachable Joining

VISUAL JOINING. Visual joining is a quick and easy method of fastening, as no tools or adhesives are required. The pieces and parts can be moved and rearranged to create changes in image. Use matching lines, dots or colors to indicate specific positions that may be needed for the assemblage. This method is suitable for toys and games.

HOLES FOR HOLDING. Use holes as holders for such linear materials as stems, branches, wire, rods or tubes. This method allows for the removal and replacement of parts and is suitable for such craft objects as tool racks (Color Plates 3 and 4), table centerpieces, or weed and candle holders. Select material that already has holes or make new ones with either a punch or drill, depending on the thickness of the material.

WEDGING. Slits or slots can be used for wedging materials together. Take advantage of any slits or cracks in the materials or make some with a knife, chisel or coping saw. Use sandpaper or a file to taper the edges of the material to be attached so that it can easily be forced into the slits and slots. This method makes a very secure hold when compressible materials like leather, cork and wood are used.

27

Joining and Fastening Methods: Permanent Fastening

PASTING AND GLUING. Select adhesives suitable for the texture and porosity of the materials to be fastened. In general, use white emulsion pastes and glues for porous materials like cardboard, cork and wood; use plastic or "china" cements for the non-porous, smooth and shiny materials like natural seashells, china, glass and plastics; use rubber cements for flexible materials like leather and rubber; and use epoxy glues to join metals and unlike materials. (See Appendix for further information on adhesive mediums and materials.)

JOINING WITH METAL FASTENERS. A wide variety of metal fasteners is manufactured for the joining of all types of materials. These can be attached with ordinary household tools. The fasteners make a secure hold and their metallic sheen and shapes also add to the visual interest of the assemblage. (See Part III for specific instructions for tools and metal fasteners for flexible and rigid materials.)

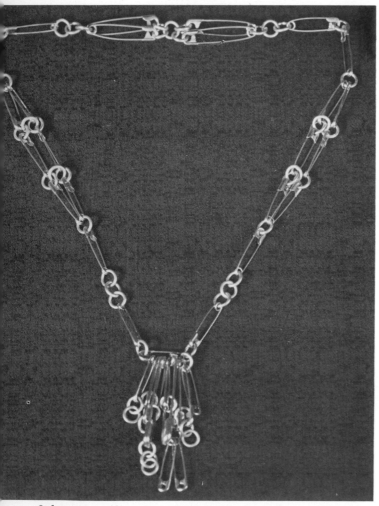

Safety pin necklace. Pins attached with wire rings.

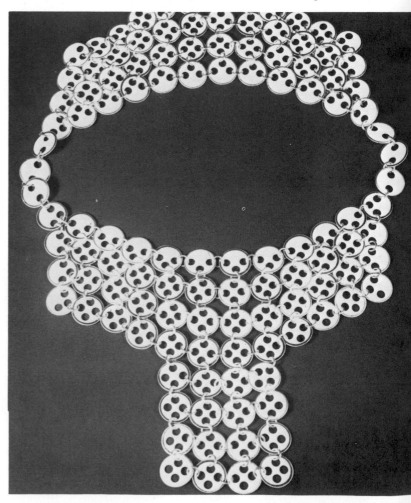

Key tag necklace. Perforated key tags attached with wire rings.

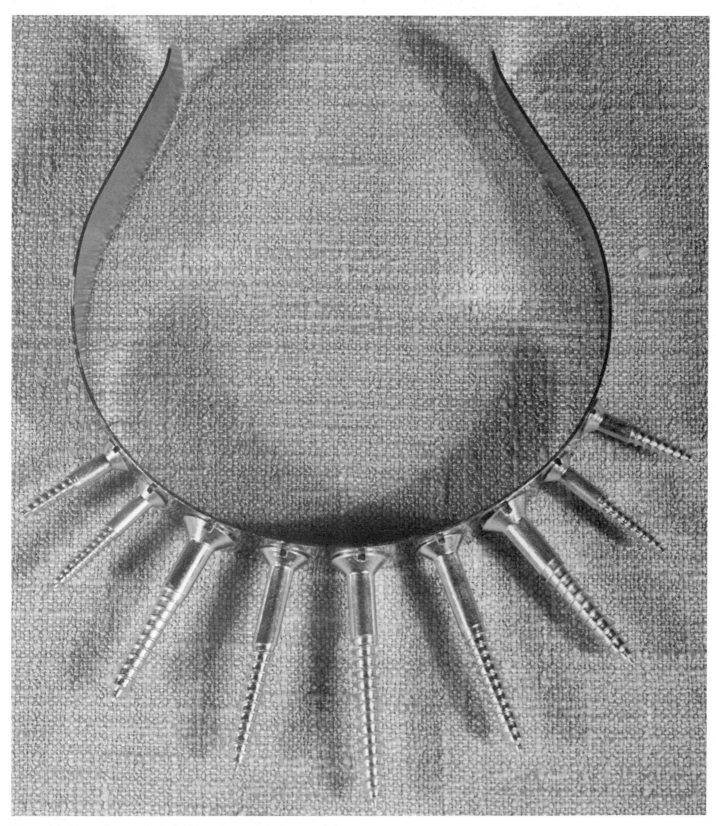

Screwy Necklace. Screws of diminishing sizes attached to steel frame with epoxy cement.

Corncob toy. Use of tape for fastening.

SEWING AND LACING. Sewing and lacing are especially suitable for the assemblage of crafts to wear, such as necklaces and belts. Use an ordinary needle with button thread to pierce and sew through natural castaways like seeds and thin flexible materials like cardboard, sheet cork and felt. To attach harder and firmer types of material, pierce or drill holes in advance; then lace through the holes with threads, cords, shoelaces, ribbons or strips of leather.

CAGING. Use wire or strips of metal or leather to make a binding "cage" around the forms of hard materials like stones, pebbles and rocks. Use a minimum of the binding material so that the forms can be seen through the caging. Attach the caged pieces together with the same binding material or use a contrasting type of cord or lacing.

TAPING. Taping is a quick way of joining many materials. Use masking tapes for temporary holding. These allow for adjustments and changes in arrangements and groupings. Use bookbinder's linen tapes or electrical insulation tapes for secure fastening.

TYING. Use cords, ropes or ribbons to wrap and tie materials together. Utilize the contrasting colors and textures of the tying materials as well as the knots and endings as a visual feature of assemblage.

EMBEDDING. Use papier-mâché pulp or strips for encasing or embedding materials such as seashells, marbles, pebbles, stones and rubber balls. When the papier-mâché is dry, it can be pierced for sewing or drilled for lacing. (See Chapter 7 for detailed instructions for papier-mâché.)

SOLDERING. Soft solders are adequate for joining tin cans and other common metal castaways. Use an electric soldering iron or propane torch. Cleaning and preliminary preparation are important. (See Chapter 7 for detailed instructions for soldering metals.)

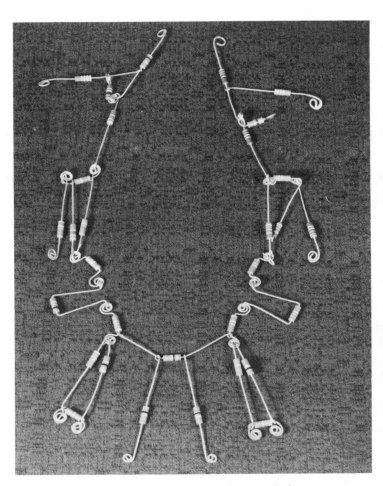

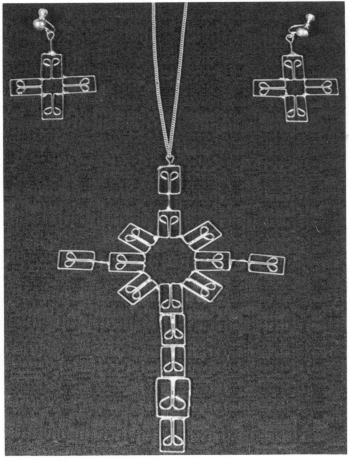

Transistor necklace. Wire shaped and hammered for decorative fastening.

Paper clip necklace and earrings. Soldered fastening.

Japanese pebble toy. No tools or adhesives are needed for visual joining.

Nature's castaways; pebbles and driftwood.

CHAPTER 3/Crafts of Nature's Castaways

Nature provides a bountiful supply of castaway material of infinite diversity. There is a myriad of different sizes, shapes, colors and textures in the seeds, shells and husks from fruits and vegetables; in the bones, furs and feathers from animals, birds and fish; and in the pebbles, rocks and shells from coastal shores.

Whatever the source, each "find" is different from all the others. In fact, no two are ever identical! The differences range from subtle variations to striking contrasts; and from amazing complexity to sheer simplicity (Color Plate 1). The combinations and formations are always unpredictable as they evolve through many years of ecological seasoning and adaptation.

The diversity of the material makes it easy for a person to choose and work with the kinds of things that really interest him. Often a single source of material provides many different choices. For example, while one person may be excited by the full blaze of colors of Indian seed corn, another might be much more interested in the subtle, muted tones of the dried corn husks that encased the corn. Similarly, one might prefer to work with the twisted, irregular forms and textures of the branch from an old oak tree while another is much more fascinated by the delicate intricacies of the inner core of the acorn. Such options for selection are an important first step to personal expression.

The availability of nature's castaways is another important asset. Such riches are usually free for the taking and can be found anywhere in some form or other. While some localities abound in pine cones and needles from evergreens, others are deluged with the fibrous peelings, husks and nuts from tropical palms. Even the desert yields its tumbleweeds, cactus spines and colorful gravel and stones.

The search for natural material doesn't necessarily involve field trips to faraway places. This can be a rewarding adventure in the heart of big cities as well as in suburban areas and the rural countryside. Trees shed their branches, bark, nuts and seeds in city parks and parkways as well as in the woods and forests. Even the few trees and single row of shrubs or bushes in a small backyard will yield an ample supply for those who have learned how to look and see.

Necklace. Polynesia; Fiji Islands. Bones, sennit, beads and fiber. Symmetrical arrangement in diminishing sizes. (Courtesy: The Museum of Primitive Art, New York.)

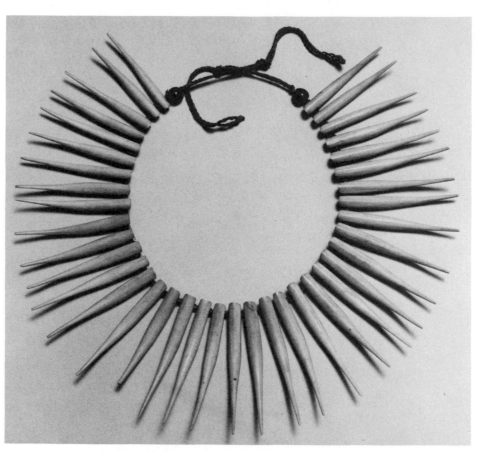

Necklace. New Mexico; Zuni. Alternate repetition of groups of shells and stones. (Courtesy: The Museum of Primitive Art, New York.)

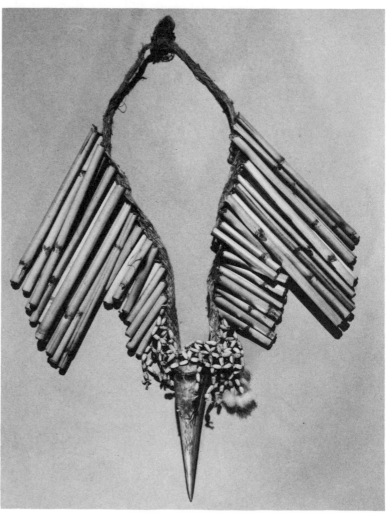

Necklace. Melanesia; New Guinea. Bamboo, fiber, seeds and hornbill. Asymmetrical arrangement of variable sizes and textures. (Courtesy: The Museum of Primitive Art, New York.)

Dance cap. Congo (Kinshasa); Bemba. Cowrie shells and boar's tusks.
Regular repetition of the same unit; symmetrical balance. (Courtesy: The
Museum of Primitive Art, New York.)

Hambone necklace. Bone segments fastened with cord shows the use of knots as a visual feature. Asymmetrical balance.

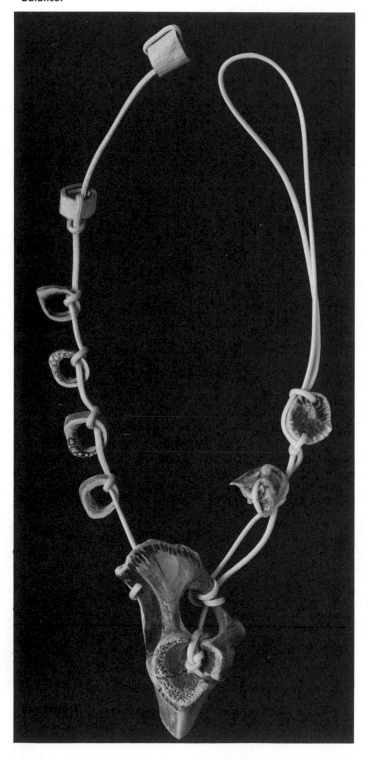

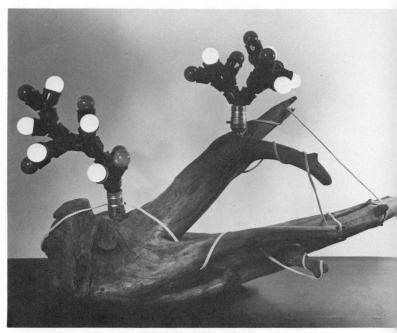

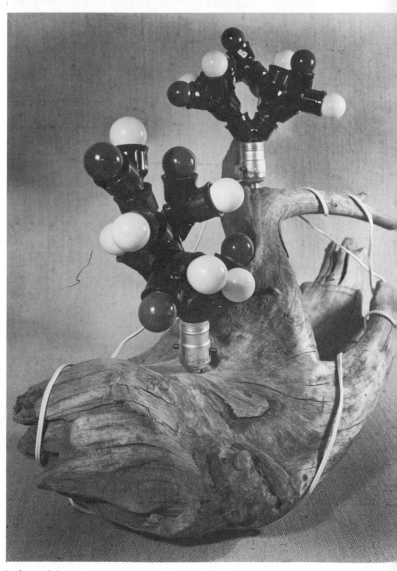

Driftwood lamp; two views. Nature's castaways combined with ready-mades. Holes are used as holders for socket rods. Natural prongs of wood are utilized for variable arrangements of electrical cord.

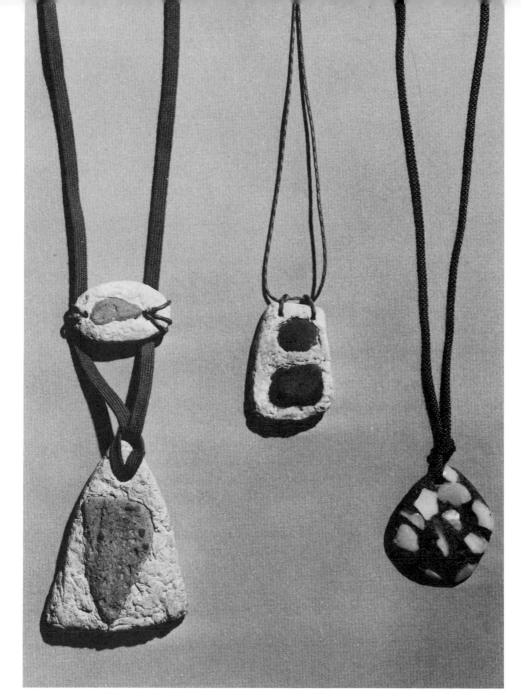

Pendants of pebbles. Pebbles are embedded in papier-mâché.

The unique qualities of natural material are not always obvious or immediately apparent. They often go unnoticed in a fast-paced world of competing stimuli. As seen in Color Plates 1 through 4, even the most striking colors and unusual formations are generally muted and subtle in contrast to the stark brilliance of the man-made materials that dominate so much of the environment. Making crafts of nature's castaways motivates new interest and curiosity about the material and can do much to develop the keen observation and sensitive discernment that are so vital to creative expression.

All in all, nature's castaways are the ideal kind of material to use as a "starter" for the crafts of assemblage. The generally casual qualities of the material do much to release any inhibitions and concerns that beginners may have about making mistakes. People feel very much at ease in using such material and dare to be themselves with it.

Teddy Bear. Castaway pipes and fittings joined with standard pipe threading.

CHAPTER 4/Crafts of Man-Made Castaways

In recent years, the overabundance of man-made castaways has zoomed to a problem of major concern in contemporary living. Numerous efforts and plans for the demolition, recycling and reuse of the material are in the offing. The primary goal of this new anxiety and activity is to find ways to get rid of the discards and clean up the environment. Artists and teachers, on the other hand, have been "recycling" castaways in creative ways for a good many years.

Artists find great delight in collecting and using "found" objects and materials for sculptural assemblage. The work of Dada and Surrealist painters and sculptors, as well as that of the contemporary Pop-Art artist, has done much to arouse interest in the use of commonplace products as a vehicle for the expression of many moods and purposes: to amuse and amaze; to shock and startle; or to ridicule and condemn.

Art teachers have long relied on the readily available and cost-free castaways for much of the three-dimensional work in the schools, particularly when the budget and supplies are limited. However, they are also finding that discarded materials are even more important because of their motivational assets. People feel comfortable with close-to-home discards. Many who are overly cautious with brand-new materials dare to work larger and more directly with castaway junk. (See Color Plates 5 through 7.) The abundance and the wide range of types of material that can be found make it possible for different people to choose entirely different assortments and collections. Each person can enjoy the pleasure of working with material that has a special meaning for him as an individual.

The most unusual types of man-made castaways are rare "finds" of the personal chattels and heirlooms sort—rocking chairs, baby buggies, dolls and other memorabilia that had been saved for several generations for sentimental reasons. These have a special kind of appeal because of their mellowed patina and nostalgic associations.

In marked contrast to the muted tones of rusty metals and weathered woods of these old-time castaways are the dazzling colors of neon brilliance that have invaded the junk yards. The increasing use of synthetic plastics for the manufacture of all kinds of products and parts is responsible for a totally new array of colors and forms that can be found.

Hardware castaways.

Containers castaways.

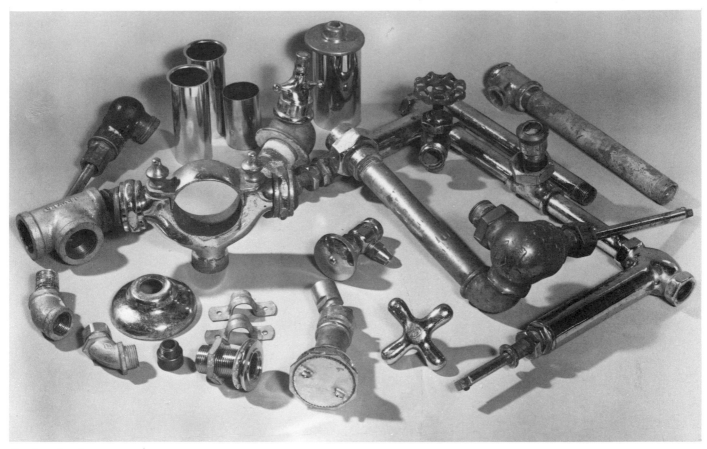

Plumbing hardware castaways.

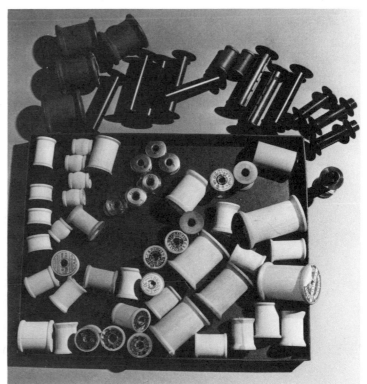

Castaway caps and spools. Each collection focuses on a single theme.

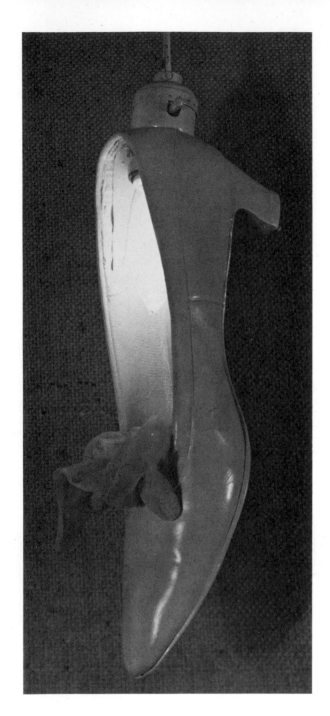

Foot Light. Old-shoe lamp using a hole as the holder for the socket and bulb.

Pencil holder utilizing ready-made holes as holders. (Courtesy: Chicago Public Schools.)

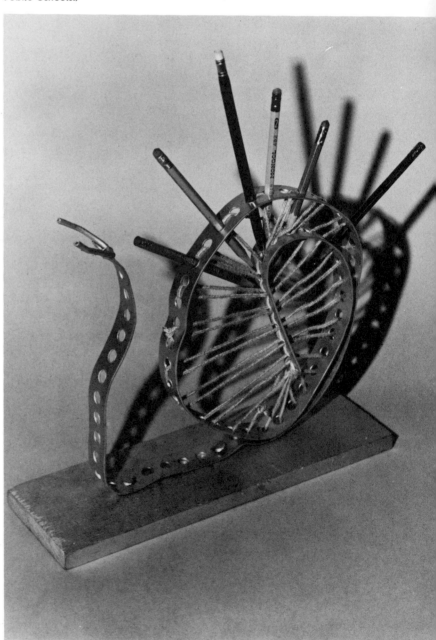

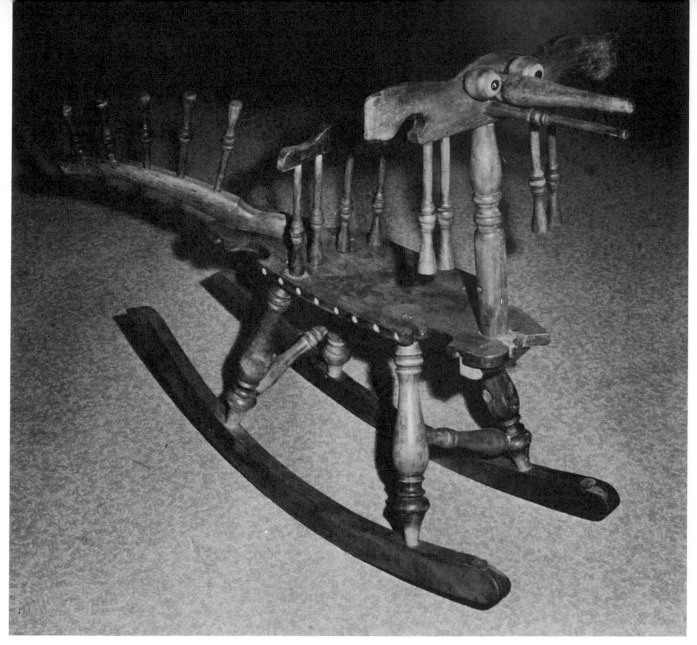

Rocking horse. Rearrangement of the pieces and parts of a castaway rocking chair.

It is also easy to find duplicates of many of these objects. There are quantities of identical egg cartons, light bulbs, film spools, pipe fittings, bottles and bottlecaps. Ideas for the adaptation and reuse of such material are often sparked by the possibilities for repetitive arrangements and groupings.

Much of the castaway junk includes various mechanical devices that were discarded for new models. There are the old clocks and timers, transistor radios, turntables, motors and countless other push-button gadgets. Many of these can be reassembled and converted to crafts of action and motion with blinking lights and changing sounds and images. It's an exciting craft project, for example, to adapt these has-been gadgets to totally new purposes such as sculptural lamps and kinetic coatracks.

The major challenge in the assemblage of man-made castaways is to find imaginative ways to give the material a new status that is dissassociated from its "has-been" role.

Colander lamp. Assemblage of kitchen castaways.

Table centerpiece. A decorative holder for napkins and silverware.

CHAPTER 5/Crafts of Ready-Mades

Ready-mades are the commonplace items that are mass-produced in anticipation of routine needs and tasks. They are the kinds of hooks, holders and fasteners that have become virtually indispensable for round-the-clock use: safety pins, paper clips, rubber bands, clothespins, curtain rings, key tags, shoe cleats, hairpins and curlers. People everywhere have learned to rely on them as the "instant" solution for countless little problems and projects every day.

Rather than having the weathered and worn look of castaway material, ready-mades are characterized by their newness and the precision of standardized production. They are available by the dozen or in prepackaged quantities of identical sameness. In fact, the most unique thing about ready-mades is that they are not unique at all!

Such material offers many practical advantages for quick craftmaking: it is cheap and easy to get in dime stores, hardware stores and supermarkets; it is new and clean and can be used immediately just "as is" without any preliminary preparation; and it is usually small and easy to handle anywhere without any special space or facilities.

The first step to motivating ideas for craft possibilities is to learn how to see the material from a new viewpoint. Since the material is so much around, people are inclined to take it for granted and become oblivious to it. For example, they don't even notice the lines and shapes that comprise the design of an ordinary safety pin. Putting such items together in totally new relationships, to serve new purposes, arouses a new awareness of the special features of the material and motivates ingenious ways to use it.

A comparison of the illustrations shows two different approaches to the use of ready-mades for craftmaking: one is to use identical items for different functions and the other is to use different kinds of items for the same function. For example, the common clothespin has been used for candleholders, letterholders, trivets and trays; and many different items such as shoe cleats, safety pins, clothespins, paper clips, horseshoe nails, screws and key tags have all been assembled into only one kind of craft object—a necklace. Both approaches allow for a wide range of individuality of expression, from the most serious and practical to lighthearted and amusing.

The straightforward simplicity of the functional design of ready-mades, which is largely due to the requirements of assembly-line production, makes them especially suitable for adaptation to new purposes. The creative individualist finds it a special challenge to transform something common and ordinary into something unusual and extraordinary.

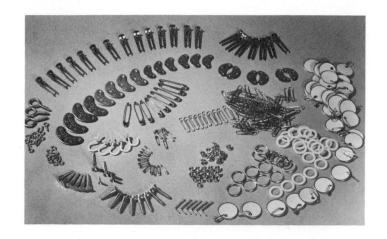

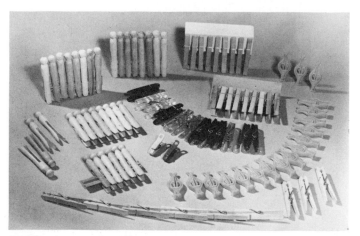

Commonplace ready-mades.

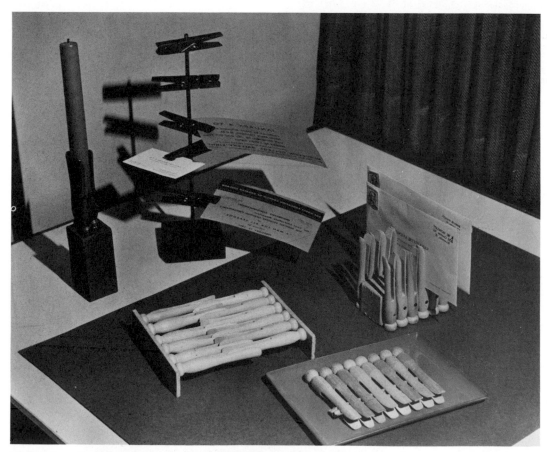

46   Clothespin crafts. Use of similar items for different functions.

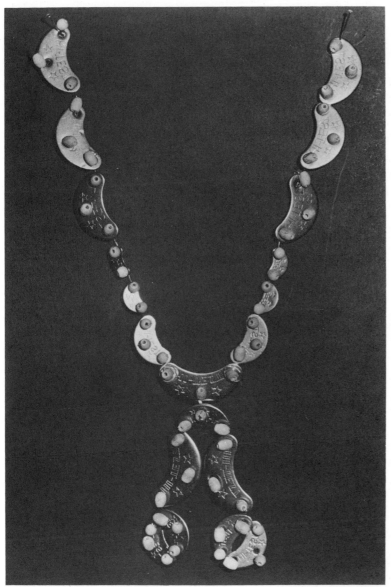

Shoe-cleat necklace. Symmetrical arrangement of shoe cleats combined with wood beads and wire. Alternate repetition of units.

Snap-fastener jewelry. Symmetrical arrangement of elements.

Plastic clothespin necklace.

47

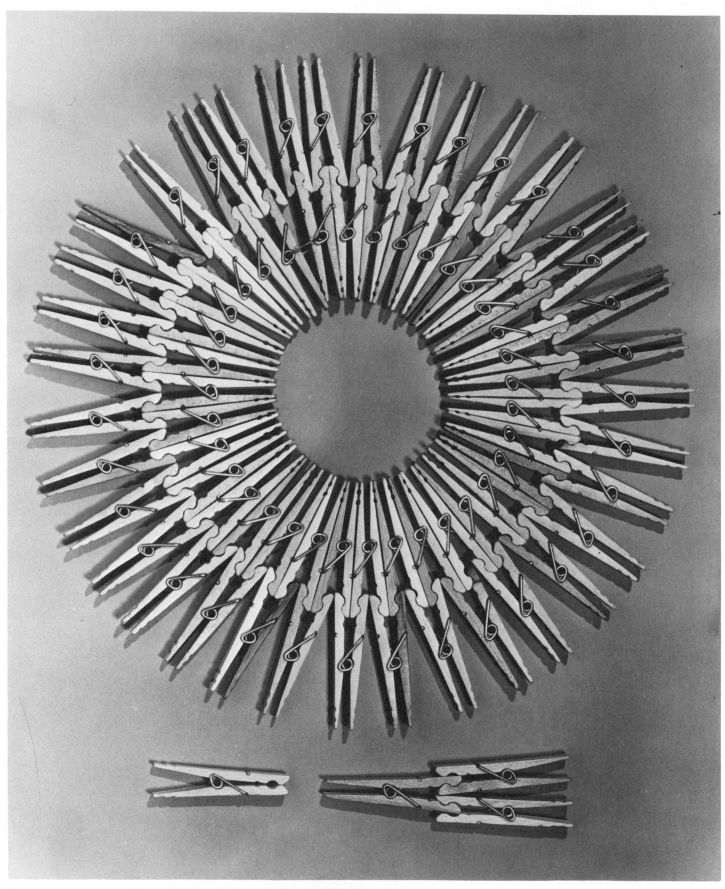

Trivet. Existing shape and form of clothes clips serve both a decorative and structural purpose. No additional materials were needed for fastening.

Stovepipe lamp.

Plastic cup lamp. Cups were attached with plastic cement.

Boudoir lamp of powder boxes. Assemblage of electrical parts and ready-mades. The base of the powder boxes was cut with a coping saw to the shape of the lamp harp. Holes were drilled to fit the bolts of standard-size lamp extenders which are used for fastening as well as decorative terminals.

49

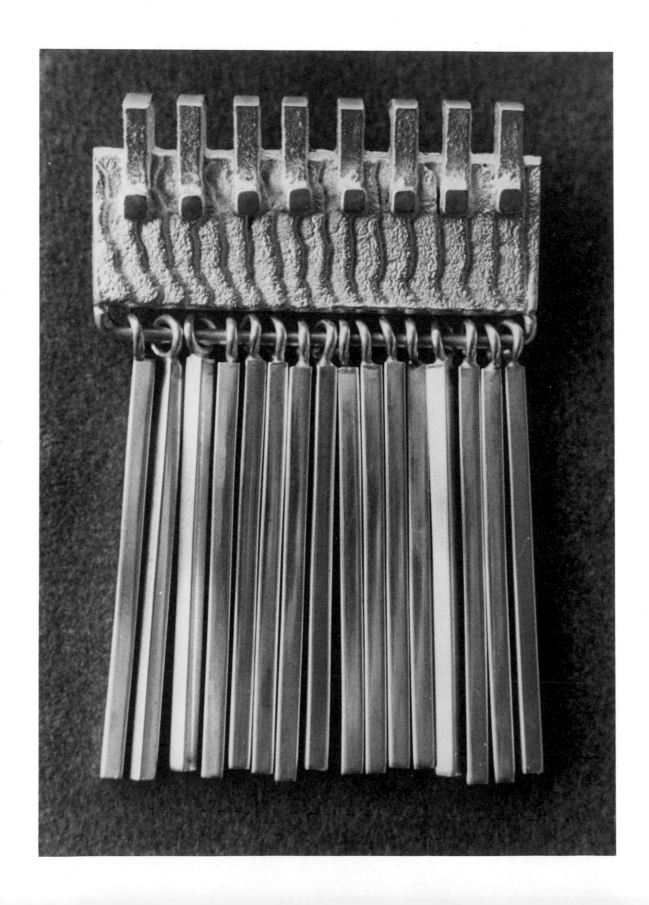

PART THREE
CRAFTS OF STRUCTURED MATERIALS

Whalebone comb. Polynesia. An example of the two basic types of edge cutting: retaining the original contour by cutting into the edge and changing the outer contour by cutting away material. (Courtesy: The Field Museum of Natural History, Chicago.)

CHAPTER 6 / Structured Materials: Definition and Processes

The primary concern in creating crafts of structured materials is with the cutting, manipulation and fastening of the materials. The purpose here is to show how to deal with these and related decorative processes in creative and individual ways. The materials approach to craftmaking is one of the most versatile and effective ways to do this. It features the exploratory and experimental use of material to nurture the conception of original ideas and personally expressive solutions to problems of design and construction. (See Color Plate 11.)

As previously noted, this approach is markedly different from one in which a prescribed pattern for a craft object is followed, step by step, to duplicate or copy a design that has already been tried and worked out by someone else. The following three-part procedure is of fundamental importance to the materials approach to craftmaking:

1. Exploration of the material to learn its inherent characteristics and qualities.
2. Experimentation with tools, materials and processes to learn the structural and decorative possibilities and limitations of the material.
3. Designing the craft object in terms of the suitability of the qualities and possibilities of the material for a specific function.

General suggestions for each step of this procedure as it relates to all types of materials are covered in the following pages. Additional instructions are given in the next three chapters for those materials which have some unique possibilities.

Exploration of the Materials

Get the facts on the source and method of production. Find out what the material is and how it is processed and fabricated. This kind of information is an important aid to learning the reasons for its distinguishing characteristics and qualities and fosters respect and appreciation for them.

Then, investigate the range of available types and forms of each material. Most materials can be fabricated in flexible sheets, rigid blocks, linear strips and rods. For example, while wood is generally a solid, rigid type of material, it is also available in paper-thin, flexible veneers; and felt and leather, which are usually flexible, can be processed in such thick and rigid forms that they can only be cut with a saw. A wide range of colors, textures, thicknesses and forms suggests more ideas for different craft possibilities. Such variety allows for more leeway in making choices and decisions on ways to use the material.

Compare each material with other similar materials. Consider its color, texture, flexibility, softness, firmness and rigidity to determine its unique qualities. Determine its advantages over similar materials as to cost, availability and usability for craft purposes.

Procure as abundant a supply of material as possible. Limited quotas of material are restrictive and inhibiting. Most material can be purchased or found in scrap form. Big piles of irregular scrap sizes and shapes are more conducive to risk-free exploration. Even if the budget is not an important factor, it is a good idea to avoid large pieces of brand-new, uniform stock, as it tends to make a person concerned about spoiling it. A well-stocked "palette" of material is just as essential to creative craftmaking as it is to creative painting. Only those who duplicate crafts from kits or copy pictures by number can get along with a minimal supply of material.

Get acquainted with the look and feel of the material. Take time to just "play" with the material to find out how it responds to touch and handling. Playful handling encourages a spontaneous response and gives people a chance to be themselves with the material. Different people have different attitudes about the same material depending on their previous experience, recollections and associations with it. Often the mere touching and handling of the material arouses the desire and interest to make something of it. This is the ideal motivational prelude for the materials approach to craftmaking.

Basic Tools and Cutting Possibilities

In general, for all types of cutting it is important to try a variety of straight, angular and curved cuts to get acquainted with the versatility of the tools and materials. To test the structural strength of the material, try cutting both simple and intricate lines and shapes; experiment to learn just how much cutting the material can withstand before it tears or breaks apart.

Three types of hand saws for edge cutting: coping saw, hacksaw and jeweler's saw. Various rigid materials have been used for experiments with edge cutting: cork, sole leather, metal, plastic and wood.

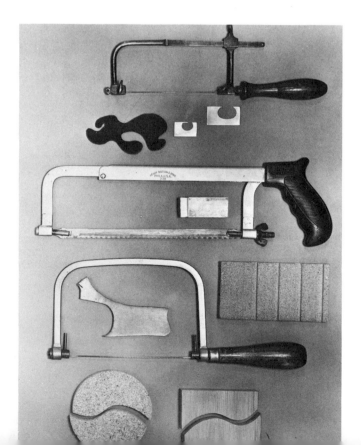

Edge cuting. The flexibility of the material determines the choice of the tool: scissors, shears or saw.

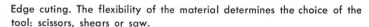

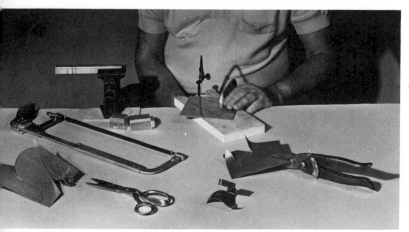

The thickness, flexibility and rigidity of the materials determines the suitability of the various tools that are suggested for use with the following methods of cutting.

EDGE CUTTING

There are two types of edge cutting. One type retains the outside shape of the material by merely cutting into the edges; none of the material is cut off, and the design is a result of only the cutting marks. The second type of edge cutting changes the outside contour of the material by cutting away shapes.

CUTTING WITH SHEARS AND KNIVES. Use ordinary scissors to cut thin weights of flexible materials such as felt, cork, leather and paper. Use tinsnips or metal-cutting shears to cut heavier weights of these same materials. If the material does not cut easily with scissors or shears, use a knife or razor blade. A mat knife is preferable for cutting firm materials that have some flexibility—such as cardboard, sheet cork and sole leather. Try freehand cutting for curved lines; use a metal-edged ruler as a guide for straight and angular cuts.

SAWING. To cut rigid materials such as metal, plastic and wood, use a saw. Coping saws and jeweler's saws with adjustable frames are versatile and can be used for small work on many different materials. For large work, use a hacksaw or wood-cutting saws. Use clamps or a vise to hold the material in a secure position for all types of sawing.

FILING. Filing is a quick way to make grooves in the edges of firm or rigid materials. Try files of various shapes and degrees of coarseness. Also use files to make rough edges smooth after sawing or cutting.

Edge cutting with an electric saber saw. Each power tool has its counterpart in a hand tool for the same function. Both hand and power tools can be used for all the basic structural processes.

Edge cutting with a power saw. The cutting marks are used to create slits and decorative patterns in various materials: cork, plastic and wood.

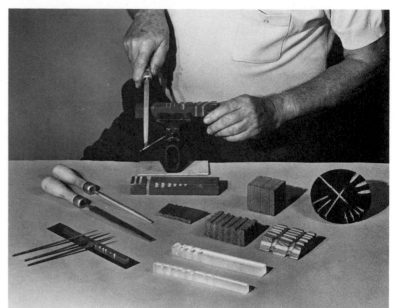

Files for filing rigid materials. The various shapes of files can be used to create curved, angular and straight-edged patterns. Experiments in cork, leather, metal, plastic and wood.

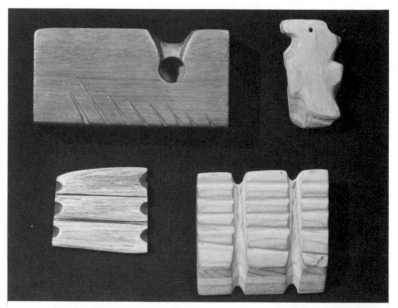

Experiments with filing wood.

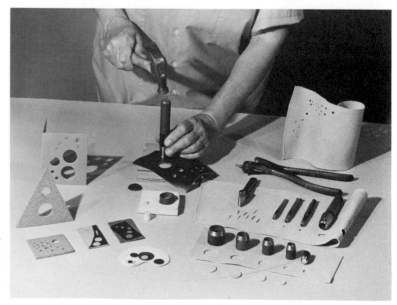

Punches for perforating flexible sheet materials. The revolving tube punch and various sizes and shapes of drive punches have been used to perforate felt, leather, paper and cork.

INTERNAL CUTTING

Internal cutting is done within the outer confines of a piece of material. Shapes of the material can be cut away completely or just partially cut and left attached at several points for various linear designs and textural effects. The following tools and methods are suitable for the different types of internal cutting.

PERFORATING. Most flexible material can be perforated with revolving tube punches. These are made in a range of diameters and leave clean-cut edges. Ordinary paper punches can only be used on very thin, firm material; they are not suitable for thicker material like felt, cork or leather, as they tear and stretch the material. Hollow drive punches are made in large diameters and oval shapes for use on all types of flexible materials. To make perforations of other shapes, use a mat knife, razor blade or chisels. To assure clean-cut edges, exert enough force to punch or cut through the material the first time; it is difficult to retrace a cut with precise accuracy. To protect the knife-sharp edges of these cutting tools, place the material on a piece of linoleum before striking the tool with a hammer.

DRILLING. To bore holes through firm or rigid materials, use drills. The bits are made in various diameters to ¼″ size. For larger holes, use a brace with auger bits. Clamp the material over a piece of linoleum to protect the work surface and the cutting edges of the drill bits. Partial drilling of the material can be used for embedding other material and also for decorative patterns.

Tools for drilling rigid materials. The hand drill and brace and bits.

Experiments with drilling. Complete, partial and tapered holes in wood, plastic and metal.

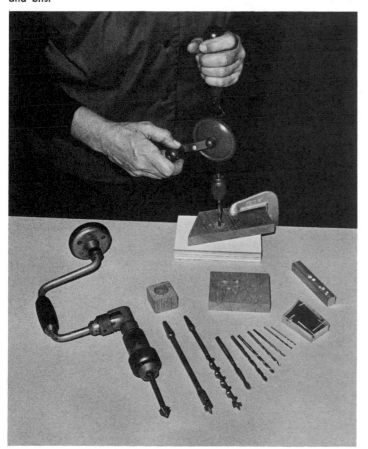

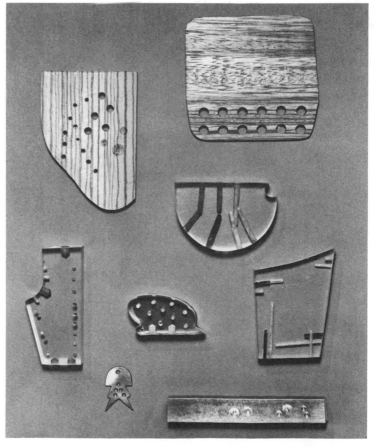

INTERNAL SAWING. For internal cutting of rigid materials, first mark the shape of the design with a pencil or scratch tool. Drill holes of about ⅛″ diameter at several points of the design where the direction changes. Insert a coping saw blade into one of the holes, and then fasten the blade to the saw frame. Clamp the material to a V-shaped board so that the saw can be used freely in an up-and-down direction. Saw all around the design from hole to hole. The inside piece of material can be cut away entirely or it can be left attached at several points.

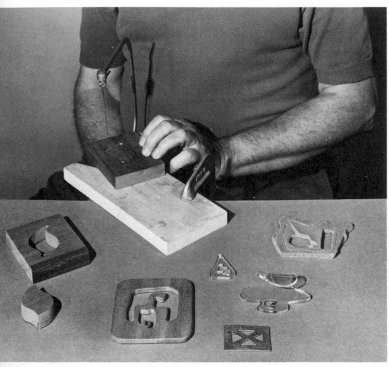

Internal sawing. Using the coping saw and V-shaped clamp board. Experiments with internal sawing of wood, cork, metal and plastic.

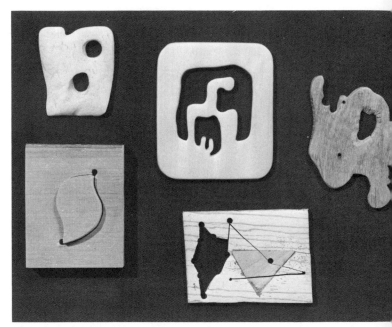

Experiments with internal sawing of wood.

SURFACE CUTTING

Surface cutting is chiefly used for decorative purposes. However, it can also be used to solve practical problems, especially when there is a need for the embedding of other material. Depressions in such surfaces can also be used as holders for numerous craft purposes.

INCISING. Incised cutting is done with sharp, pointed tools. Any firm or rigid material can be used. For delicate lines, use a scriber or any pointed tool like an awl or center punch. For deeper grooves, retrace the design with a gouge or chisel. To prevent the work from sliding when the thrust of a tool is applied, clamp a block of wood to the worktable for use as a bench stop. This serves the same purpose as a clamp or vise but allows for more freedom to move the material around. Try various depths and types of lines: uniform, accented, jagged and irregular.

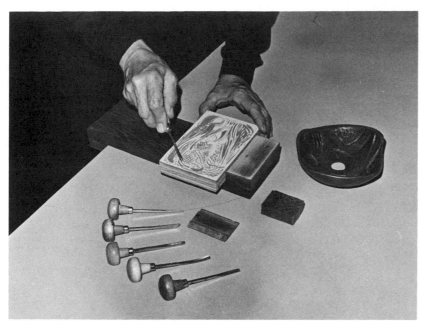

Surface cutting. Gouges and chisels used for incising and relief carving.

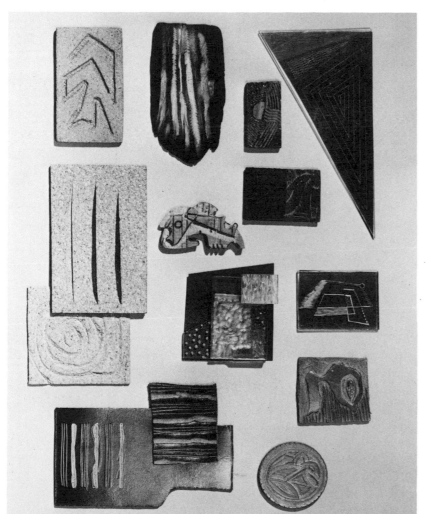

Experiments with incising and relief carving of various materials: cork, wood, plastic and leather.

Comb. New Guinea. Bamboo; 12½" long. An example of edge cutting and incising. (Courtesy: The Museum of Primitive Art, New York.)

RELIEF CARVING. Relief carving is used to project shapes from the background. In surface cutting, the degree of projection is slight. First, outline the entire design by incising. Then, use a gouge or chisel to cut away either the background or the shape of the design.

THREE-DIMENSIONAL CARVING

Use blocks of material that are at least 1″ to 2″ thick. Any and all types of cutting tools can be used, depending on the size and type of material. For example, even a small pocketknife or razor blade can be used to carve small blocks of wood, cork or plastic.

Gouges and chisels, which are made in a diversity of curved and angular shapes, are ideal for most types of carving. Use a bench stop or clamp the material to a worktable or hold it in a vise. For quick cutting of large blocks, use a mallet and chisels. Use drills and auger bits to make holes and deep cuts within the material and a saw to cut away large areas along the edges. Use files and sandpaper for smooth surfacing.

FOUR-DIMENSIONAL CARVING

Four-dimensional carving is a means of achieving action and motion. It involves cutting away material in such a way that pieces and parts can be moved about within it.

Use drills and chisels to remove material from within the core of the block. Do this cautiously and sparingly until the center portion of the block is encased or caged within the outer confines of the block and can be moved around by shaking or twisting.

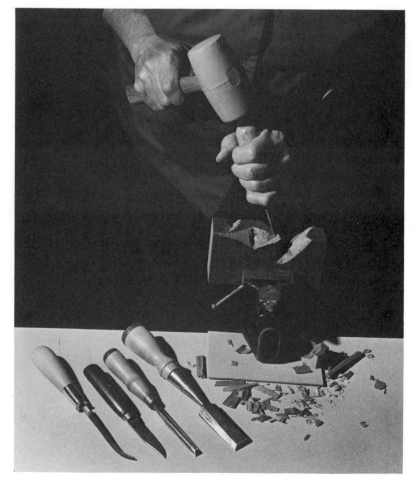

Wood experiments showing various techniques of carving.

Carving tools: knives, gouges and chisels. With the block of wood held securely in a vise, both hands are free to use a mallet and chisel for three-dimensional carving.

Carving of salt blocks; two views of an additive structure. Detachable joining allows for four-dimensional changes in position of the oval form by matching concave and convex surfaces.

(Below) An example of four-dimensional carving.

(Left) Carving of salt blocks; two subtractive structures. Three-dimensional carving of identical salt blocks in distinctly individual ways.

61

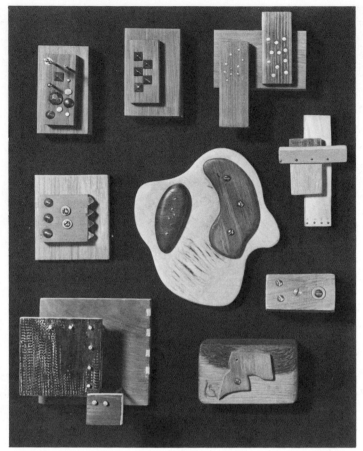

Structures of wood with surface overlays fastened
with nails and screws.

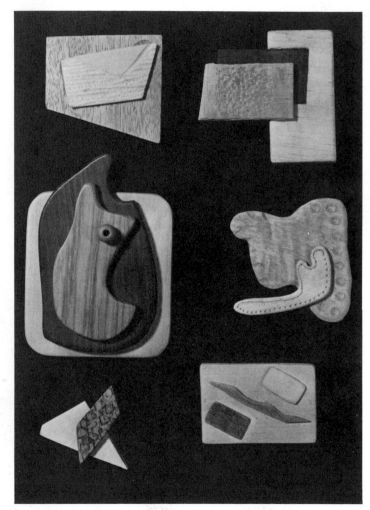

Structures of wood with surface overlays fastened
with adhesives.

Fastening Possibilities for Additive Structures

SURFACE OVERLAYS. Overlays are a quick way to join two or more
pieces of material to make relatively flat structures of low relief. Use
adhesives, metal fasteners, sewing, lacing or dowel rods to attach the
pieces together. This is a type of laminating which adds strength and
support to the material. For visual interest, use contrasting shapes,
sizes, colors and textures. Also, try overlay extensions beyond the base
material.

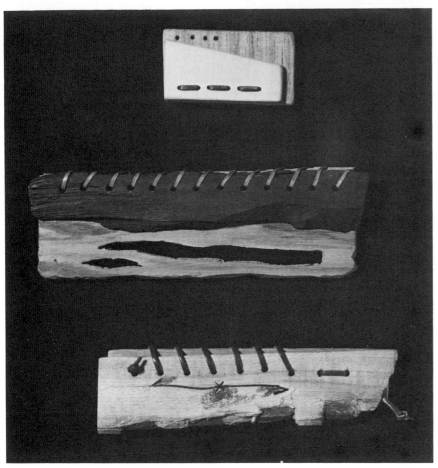

Pieces of wood fastened by means of lacing.

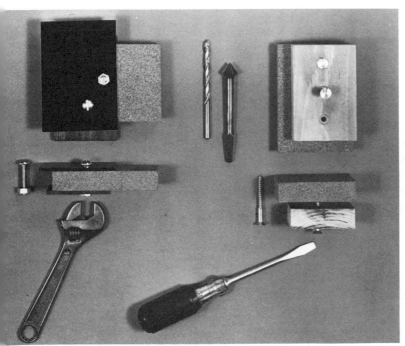

Surface overlays of various materials: plastic, cork and wood. Fastening with screws and bolts.

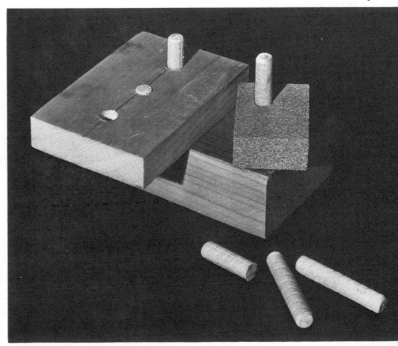

Fastening with wood dowel rods.

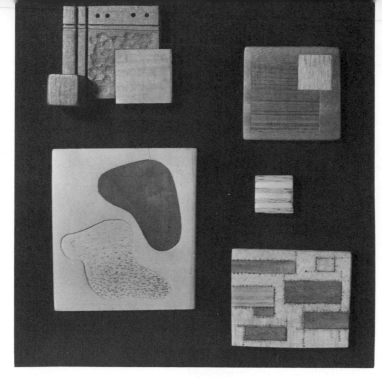

Surface inlays using wood. Various methods of cutting and embedding.

SURFACE INLAYS. Inlay involves the cutting and insertion of contrasting materials into the body of the surface. It is primarily used as a means of adding to the visual interest of the material. However, it also has practical advantages where a change in textural surface from rough to smooth or shiny to dull may be needed.

Use adhesives to fasten the pieces. To assure a flat surface, place the material under pressure to prevent warping. There are several methods of cutting material for inlay. The choice depends on the thickness of the material and the ultimate purpose.

Perforating is the quickest method of cutting flexible material for inlay. Use punches to perforate the base material. Save the cutouts; then, change their color or texture before replacing them in the perforated base. Any other contrasting material of the same thickness as the base can also be used to replace the cutouts. Attach the entire work to another piece of material as a support.

Internal sawing can be used for inlaying of firm, rigid materials that are at least ⅛″ thick. Change the color or texture of the cutouts or duplicate their size and shape in another material of the same thickness. Before replacing the cutouts, use a thin coating of glue to attach them to the edges of the cuts. If the material is more than ¼″ thick, it is not necessary to attach the work to another base for support.

All-over cutting is another method of making an inlaid structure. Use a design that extends to all the edges of the piece of material. Cut the entire design apart as for a jigsaw puzzle. Change the color, texture or surface pattern of alternate pieces and replace them. Use adhesives for permanent attachment or leave the pieces separate for detachable joining.

Surface removal is the most difficult method of cutting material for inlaid designs. However, it does make a durable structure. Use firm material that is at least ¼″ thick. Cork, leather and wood are suitable. Outline the design with a knife or sharp, pointed tool. Cut away the surface to a depth that will accommodate the thickness of the material to be embedded.

SURFACE PROJECTION. For the spatial projection of surfaces, arrange the pieces of thin rigid material as for overlays, but attach them so that there is space between them. Use nails, pegs, rods or wire to simultaneously attach and project the surfaces at different levels. The space itself becomes an important part of the structure and can be used for both visual interest and numerous functional purposes.

ANGULAR JOINING. Angular joining is the most versatile and widely used method of structuring rigid material. Use slits, slots or holes for a quick method to support pieces in various angular positions. This method allows for adjustments and rearrangements. It involves the insertion of one piece of material through an opening in another piece.

To fasten material at right angles to a base or for corner structures, cut the pieces to a precise fit at the place of attachment. Use adhesives, nails or screws, depending on the thickness and porosity of the material. When fastening hard or brittle materials with nails or screws, drill a hole slightly smaller than the shaft of the nail or screw to prevent splitting of the material.

The interlocking of two pieces of material is one of the most secure methods of angular attachment. It is generally used to join material at right angles for corners; it can also be used for many other types of three-dimensional structures. It involves cutting and fitting of positive projections and negative openings. The traditional methods of dovetailed joining are an example of interlocking. However, the same principle can be used to make more imaginative and inventive structures by changing the sizes, shapes and placement of the projections and openings.

(Above) Joining featuring surface projection of parallel planes.

(Right) Examples of angular joining: interlocking and wedging.

Mobile structure of cork and wire.

Mobile of metal by Alexander Calder. (Courtesy: The Arts Club of Chicago.)

Possibilities for Action and Motion

MOBILE STRUCTURES

Mobile structures are generally characterized by ease of movement. They respond quickly to the slightest stimuli—touch of the hand or even gentle winds. They make variable movements and arrangements as well as sounds of tinkling or clanging, depending on the materials used.

Use any of the cutting methods to make shapes or forms of either flexible or rigid materials: paper, cardboard, cork, metal, plastic or wood. Punch or drill holes in the material or add screw eyes or swivel hooks. Use wire or cords or rods through the holes or hooks to suspend the pieces from the ceiling or from a wall or pedestal.

KINETIC STRUCTURES

In kinetic structures, the motion is generally controlled or set to a prescribed pattern of action. Wheels, rockers, hinges, levers, pulleys and magnets are the types of devices that can be used to set movable parts to action. They can be made to roll back and forth, slide up and down, or to open and close. They respond to pushing and pulling or force and pressure. Changes in position can be achieved manually or by various mechanical devices such as motors, switches and timers.

Visually, the design must be planned in such a way that the pieces and parts are interesting in both stopped and moving positions or when they are separated and placed in new arrangements.

(Far Left) *Jackpop.* Kinetic structure. (Courtesy: Creative Playthings, Inc.)

(Left) *Cat and Canary.* Paper sculpture featuring cutting and manipulation of the material.

(Below) Toy cow. Leather and wood. Cutting and manipulation of sheet material.

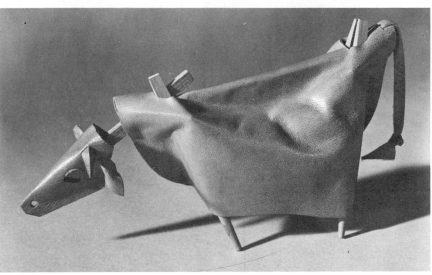

Manipulative Possibilities of Materials

SHEET MATERIAL. Flexible sheets of material such as cork, felt, leather, metal, paper and plastic can be manipulated by bending, creasing, folding and rolling. Avoid "forcing" the material to behave in a way that does not come easily. Give the material a chance. To make sharp edges for folding, score the material by using a knife or blade to cut halfway through the thickness of the material; then, bend it away from the cut. The range of manipulative possibilities can be increased by edge cutting, fold cutting and semi-perforating. These preliminary cuts make it possible to do one-piece structures that are manipulated from within the sheet itself. Since no material is cut away and no adhesives are needed, the result is sturdy and durable.

To manipulate heavy sheet material such as cork, leather and plywood, soak it in water until it is pliant. After forming and shaping it, hold it in position with binding tapes or clamps until dry.

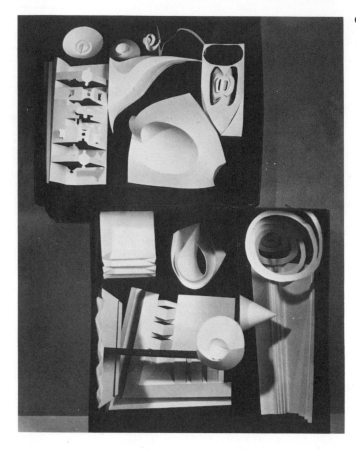

Cutting and manipulation of paper after scoring.

Manipulation of sheet material: metal, cork, leather and wood veneer. Scoring and cutting facilitates creasing, folding and bending.

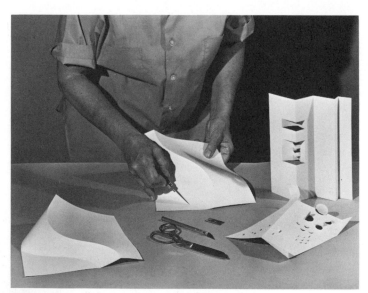

Manipulation of paper after scoring. Edge cutting and semi-perforating increase the range of manipulative possibilities.

Cutting and manipulation of heavy sheet material after soaking in water. Tape is used to hold material in position until it is dried.

68

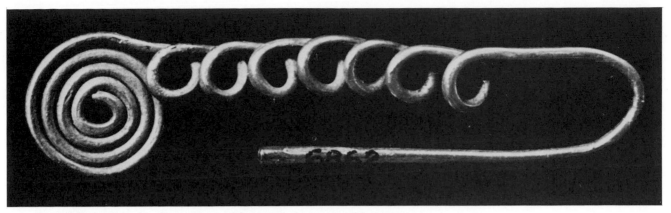

Hairpin. Colombia. Decorative and functional object created by manipulating a single piece of wire. (Courtesy: The Field Museum of Natural History, Chicago.)

LINEAR MATERIAL. Flexible materials of linear form such as cord, rope, raffia, reed and lacings of leather and plastic are especially suitable for such manipulative possibilities as tying, knotting, braiding and coil binding. Most of these techniques can be done entirely by hand, as only scissors and needles may be needed to start and to finish the work. Try both flat and three-dimensional structures. To build up forms, use overlapping or coil binding. Also, try wrapping linear materials over a foundation form, such as a can, bottle or carton. Attach the material to the foundation by binding, sewing or pasting. Flexible rods of wire can be manipulated into self-supporting forms without any binding or fastening.

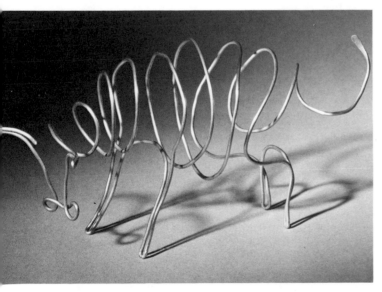

(Left) Wire bull. Manipulation of wire in continuous line designs makes self-supporting structures without any binding or fastening.

(Below) Japanese oshibori. Manipulation of linear material; tying and binding of bamboo strips.

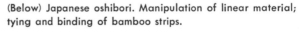

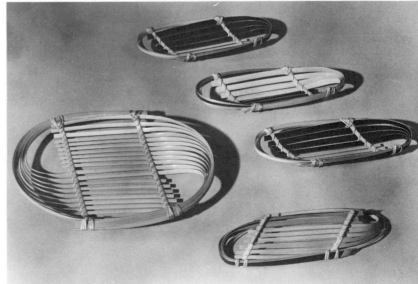

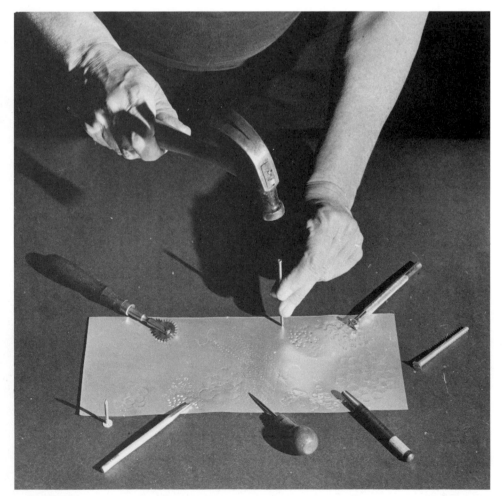

Surface treatment: metal, wood and leather. Texturing by pricking, hammering and stamping.

Frontlet and mouth-plate. Gold foil. Cypriote, Late Bronze Age (1500–1200 B.C.) Surface treatment by tooling and stamping. (Courtesy: The Metropolitan Museum of Art. The Cesnola Collection.)

Decorative Possibilities: Surface Treatment

TEXTURING. Textural changes can be used to achieve contrasts for visual interest as well as for practical purposes. For example, a roughened surface makes for a firmer grip. For hard-surfaced materials, such as metal, plastic and close-grained woods, use a knife, chisel or pointed tool for scratching, piercing and pricking. Multiple cuts along a ruler edge make a sharply defined textural pattern. For firm, impressionable materials like leather, cardboard, porous wood and soft sheet metals, use steel stamping and modeling tools. Flathead screws and large-headed nails make a good substitute. For hammered textures, use a ball peen hammer or round dapping dies.

Chessmen. Algerian, 18th Century. Texturing of copper and brass by hammering and stamping. (Courtesy: The Metropolitan Museum of Art. Gift of Gustavus A. Pfeiffer, 1953.)

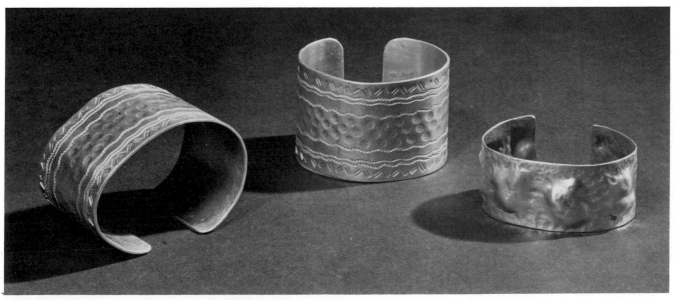

Bracelets of flexible metal. Two types of surface treatment: patterns from steel stamping tools and stretching of metal by hammering.

COLORING. The suitability of the coloring medium depends on the porosity and texture of the material and the functional purpose. Wax mediums such as colored crayons and colored pencils are quick and effective to use on papers, cork, felt and porous woods. Liquid mediums such as dyes, inks and paints are more versatile for use on many different materials because of the variety of binders that are used in their manufacture. To determine the coloring possibilities of any dry or liquid medium, work for a wide range of opposites in effects. Experiment with applications from thick to thin and from light to dark. Try various applicators such as pens, pencils and fine brushes for fine details and linear designs; try sponges, cloths, large brushes, spatter guns and aerosol sprayers for large masses and background areas. In general, it is wise to keep the coloring mediums (as well as other decorative treatments) subordinate, to avoid concealing the inherent textural quality of the material. (See Color Plate 27.)

Surface coloring. Dry and liquid mediums and methods of application.

Surface burning. The electric burning tool used in experiments on cork, leather and wood.

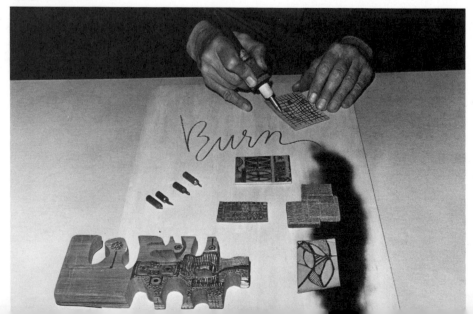

BURNING. Surface burning is a means of changing both the color and texture of the material. The results are permanent and durable because they become an integral part of the surface. Electric wood-burning tools are made with interchangeable points of different sizes and shapes. They can be used on many other materials as well as on wood: cork, leather, paper and plastic. Try various weights and pressures to create patterns of dots, lines and shapes. Use the flat-edge points for broad strokes and make a gradation of tones from light to dark. For large areas of tone, use a propane torch.

Coating with colorless mediums.

COATING AND FINISHING. Colorless coatings such as wax, shellac, varnish and lacquer are primarily used as a protective finish. However, they can also be used for visual contrasts. Experiment with a range of opposites from the most subtle sheen of wax and dull varnish to the highest gloss of shiny varnish and lacquer. The amount of gloss is partly due to the amount of resin in the medium and partly a result of the number of coats applied.

Shellac, varnish, lacquer and wax add a protective coating and show variations in tone and sheen in the different materials: cardboard, leather, metal, composition boards and wood.

Experiment with surface coating of wood.

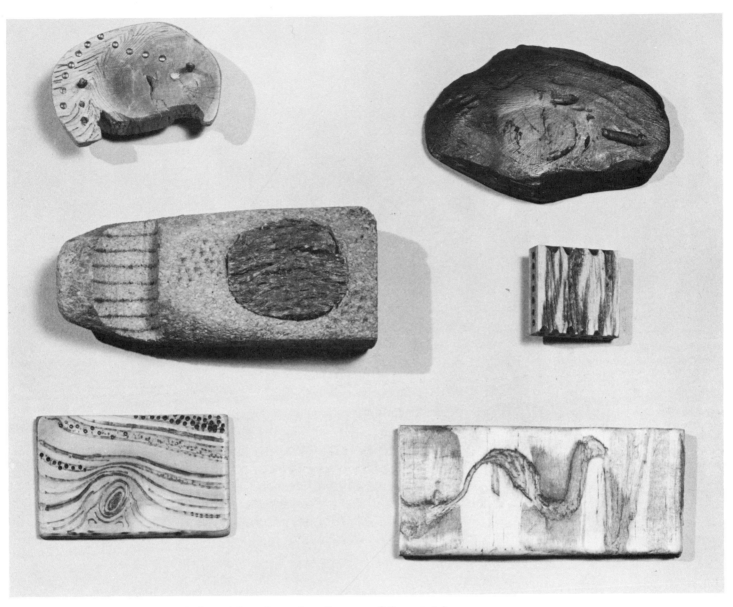

Material motifs derived from the grain and texture of the materials.

Design Possibilities: Pattern Motifs

MATERIAL MOTIFS. Material motifs are the result of the natural growth or processing of materials. Many materials have a dominant and striking pattern of their own—the result of their natural grain, texture or color. It is wise to utilize these as a design motif instead of imposing another competing pattern over them. For example, the grain and shapes of knots, burls and growth rings in many woods can be used as the starting point for a decorative design motif. Emphasize the lines and shapes by retracing them with a dot or line design. Highlight them with a shiny coating or rub in a contrasting color to reveal them. Similarly, the natural creases in a skin of leather can be emphasized by tooling or stamping. The patterns of natural cork grain can be repeated as a design motif by burning.

Material motifs inspired by the knots and irregular forms of driftwood.

Structural motifs derived from fastening. Decorative patterns of nails, screws, eyelets, rivets, stitches and lacing: cork, leather, paper, plastic, wood.

STRUCTURAL MOTIFS. Structural motifs are derived from the lines, shapes and textures that are a result of the cutting, fastening and manipulation of the materials. (See Color Plate 9.) For example, these include the shapes and shiny luster of metal fasteners such as nails, screws, snaps and eyelets, the repetitive patterns of stitches, lacing, braiding and knotting, and the visual patterns that result from interlocking, wedging and doweling. All such structural elements can be featured as decorative motifs. Show them off; don't conceal them!

GEOMETRIC MOTIFS. Motifs that are based on simple geometric shapes are preferable for experimentation with decorative possibilities, because they do not distract attention from the material or process at hand. Try arrangements of dots, lines and tones in circles, squares, rectangles and triangles. These basic geometric shapes, and slight variations of them, provide an almost unlimited source of pattern possibilities. Experiment with some precise, carefully measured arrangements and some that are casually scattered and informal. Also, try various types of lines: uniform, accented, continuous and overlapping.

SUBJECTIVE MOTIFS. Subjective motifs are adapted from nature by simplifying the shapes and forms of the subject to show its most distinguishing features. It is a special challenge to see how much of the subject can be identified with a minimum of lines. Work directly from nature or from close-up photographs. Choose familiar subjects: animals, birds, fish and insects, or flowers, leaves, fruits and vegetables. Adapt the realism of the subject to the nature of the material in accord with what "happens" in the process of cutting, texturing or coloring. Don't force the subject on the material.

Geometric motifs and variations: circles, squares, rectangles and triangles.

Subjective motifs derived from nature: animals, birds, figures and faces in various materials.

Expressional Design for Crafts

Design for craftmaking involves the organization and arrangement of all parts of the structure so that it is both functional and visually interesting. The purpose here is to consider three different approaches to design that are conducive to the creative conception of original ideas and individuality of expression: experimental, preplanned and spontaneous. These make allowance for the wide-ranging differences in attitudes, desires and interests, as well as capabilities, of different people.

EXPERIMENTAL DESIGN. This approach features the direct conversion of the experiment itself into a useful craft object. This is one of the quickest ways to make the break from stereotyped designs for crafts. Designs that emanate from the risk-free experimentation without any utilitarian restrictions are more apt to be original and directly expressive of the individual. This method is an effective transitional step from pure experimentation to practical application of experimental knowledge.

Here are some suggestions for the conversion of experiments. First, consider a diversity of uses for the experiment. Study the shape and form of the experiment. Size it up from different viewpoints. Play with it at random. Have fun! Try to adapt it into something functional just "as is," with little or no alterations. A lighthearted attitude and sense of humor are a big help; they do much to spark the imagination. For example, try the experiment out as a holder. Look for all kinds of things around the house that need holders: letters, bills, candles and flowers, scarves, ties and belts; soap, cosmetics, towels and combs; eyeglasses and costume jewelry. (See Color Plate 21.)

Consider the proportions. Avoid a "tacked-on" look. The sizes, shapes and forms of any additional material should have some kinship to the proportions of those of the experiment. In designing the holder, for example, consider the things to be held as a vital part of the design arrangement. The visual quality of the design is determined by the relationship between the holder and what is held.

Finally, choose materials that are practical for the use. An experiment made of plastic would make a suitable holder for wet things like soap and damp towels. However, a cork structure would not be practical for adaption to an ashtray because cork burns easily.

PREPLANNED DESIGN. In the preplanned approach to design, the motivation usually stems from a person's need or desire for a specific kind of object such as a belt, bag, box, tray or lamp. The problems that may be involved in structuring the object are anticipated, and an exact course of procedure for solving them is plotted in advance. This approach eliminates many of the hazards of chance mistakes and does save materials. The following procedure and suggestions have proved helpful and efficient in the preplanning of original designs for crafts.

Make some quick, rough sketches to develop ideas. Try different arrangements and combinations of the sizes, shapes and forms that could be used for the specific purpose. Play with variable possibilities. Work rapidly and freely so that one idea leads to another. Casual scribbles are better than precise drawings. Avoid finality at this point. If a person has only a single idea of the way to make the object, it is likely that it is something he has seen done before.

Experiment in wood, with edge cutting, internal sawing, and drilling, was given a wax finish and converted into a matchbook holder.

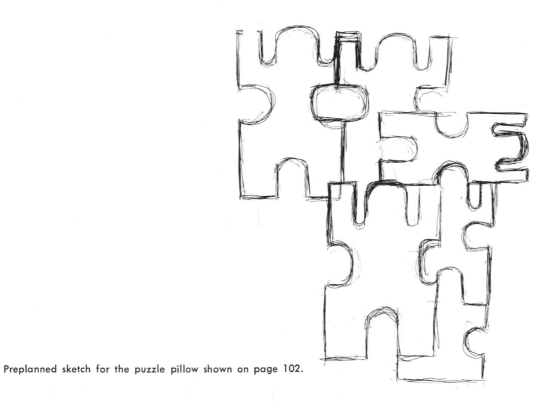

Preplanned sketch for the puzzle pillow shown on page 102.

Consider various materials suitable for the ideas. Study previous experiments with similar materials to determine which materials and processes could be used for the specific function.

Make preliminary patterns. Take time to consider all the pieces and parts that will be needed to structure the object. Make patterns of them in actual size to determine how much material is needed. Use wrapping paper for patterns for flexible materials; muslin for drapable materials; and cardboard for firm materials.

Make specific experiments. Try out on a small section of material each of the cutting and fastening methods that will be needed to carry out the design. Use materials that are identical to those that are to be used for the final piece of work. If these specific experiments are not entirely satisfactory, try alternate possibilities. Don't take chances. Find solutions in advance.

SPONTANEOUS DESIGN. The spontaneous approach to design features direct work on the final craft object. The emphasis is on an emotional and intuitive response to the material at hand. An individual's personal interests, coupled with his own reaction to the material, trigger his ideas for things to make. For example, the same piece of leather might suggest pillows and pouches to one person, a camera case or portfolio to another, and a belt or sandals to still another.

Start with the carefree handling of materials. Rely on the nature of the material to motivate ideas for the types of things that could be made of it. Make some quick rough sketches of anything that comes to mind.

Plan as you go. Consider various possibilities for structuring the shapes and forms as a whole. Don't be concerned about any details until the structure is well on its way. Rely on previous experimentation with similar materials to make decisions for the cutting and joining processes that are needed to make the object functional.

Keep an open outlook. Be alert for ways to make adjustments to take advantage of the things that "happen to happen" as the work progresses. (See Color Plates 15, 17, and 37.)

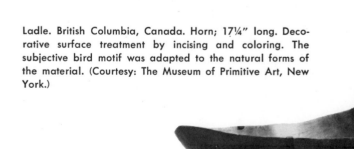

Ladle. British Columbia, Canada. Horn; 17¼" long. Decorative surface treatment by incising and coloring. The subjective bird motif was adapted to the natural forms of the material. (Courtesy: The Museum of Primitive Art, New York.)

2. Assemblage of nature's castaways. Experimentation with fastening possibilities.

1. Nature's castaways of unpredictable formations.

3. Tool rack assemblage showing detachable joining using holes as holders.

4. Sculptural tool rack.

5. Wall Hanging. Assemblage of castaway fabrics. (Courtesy: Syosset High School, New York.)

6. *Toy Cyclist*. Castaway coat hanger and springs joined with wire. Liquid plastic was applied over the wire frame of the figure. (Courtesy: Chicago Public Schools.)

7. *Kinetic Toy*. Old clock and castaway hardware parts were joined with epoxy cement. (Courtesy: Chicago Public Schools.)

9. Felt hanging with geometric and structural motifs. The surface overlays were fastened with decorative stitchery.

10. *Puzzle Pillow*, showing change in placement of parts. (Compare with illustration, page 102.)

8. *Take-off on Tiffany*. The design for cutting of carpet remnants was carefully planned for accurate fitting over the shade frame and wood base. The contrasting colors of binding tape and fringing were planned for both structural and decorative purposes.

11. Composition created out of felt experiments with cutting, fastening, manipulation and surface treatment.

12. Felt experiments adapted to lapel pins. Geometric and subjective pattern motifs.

13. *Soft Toys.* Felt forms were created using spontaneous edge cutting, fringing and decorative sewing.

14. Felt boots. An example of creative mispairment. The processes involved were manipulation, edge cutting, and fastening with overlays and decorative stitchery.

15. *Pink Lady*. An example of spontaneous design, this life-size felt toy features casual cutting and sewing. It is stuffed with cotton batting.

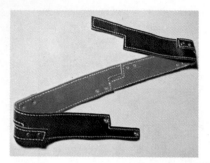

16. Leather belt. Calfskin lined with suede, featuring saddle stitching and rivets as structural motifs for decoration.

17. Leather scarf and bag. The leather was spontaneously cut and fastened with a responsive feel for the natural patterns and shapes of the skins and fragments of fur.

18. *Doggie Toys.* Stuffed leather forms of preplanned design. The designs evolved gradually from casual scribbles.

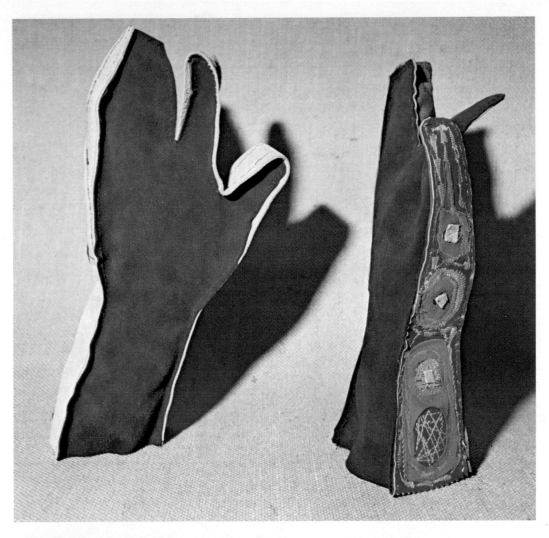

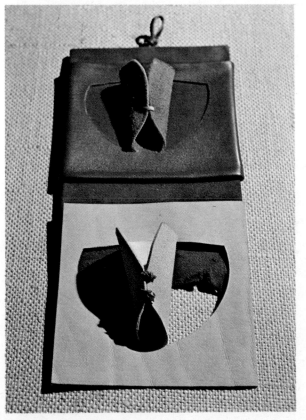

19. Sculptural mittens of suede and glazed leathers. Mispairment was pre-planned as the feature of the structural forms. Decorative stitchery was freely used.

20. Leather experiment with internal cutting, manipulation and lacing.

21. Leather pipe holder. The structural design was directly inspired by the experiment.

22. Papier-mâché by Donna Sved. Rolled paper was combined with a collage of papers, beads, cords and ribbon.

23. *Marilyn the Doll.* In this example of papier-mâché, tissue paper was draped over a cardboard foundation.

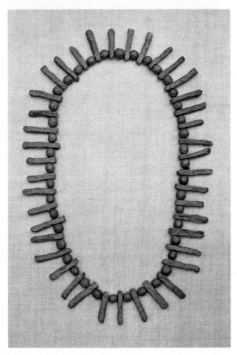

24. Papier-mâché necklace. The beads are of paper pulp.

25. Necklaces of papier-mâché beads and bamboo segments.

26. Pin cushion of papier-mâché by Gemma Taccogna, Mexico. This object shows the wide range of textural finishes that can be achieved with the paper pulp method. Fine paper pulp and several coats of lacquer make the smooth glossy finish.

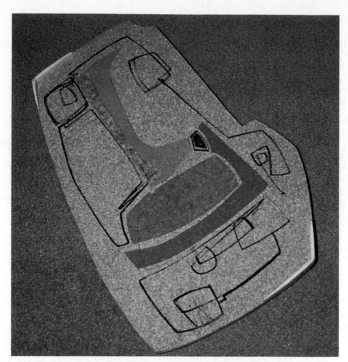

27. Wood tray inlaid with cork. The spontaneous line design emphasizes a face motif and unifies the inlaid shapes of various cork textures. The reverse side is shown on page 143.

28. Dry weed holder. Laminated cork and wood. The material was arranged with a sensitive appreciation for the contrasting textures and thicknesses. Coarse filing was used for a surface treatment that relates to the texture of weeds.

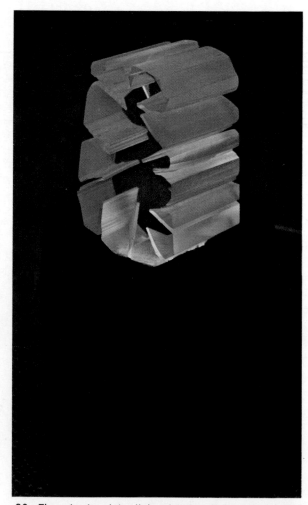

29. Plastic night light. The edge-cut plastic form was placed over a small opening in the wood box which encases the electric lamp bulb.

30. The plastic night light showing light transmission. Plexiglass conducts light invisibly through polished surfaces to any cut surfaces.

31. Plastic sand timer. A structure for color transmission and, in reversing its position, a structure of motion. (See reverse position, page 135.)

32. Plastic necklace. Sand, metallic powder and metal fasteners were embedded in liquid plastic for decorative and structural purposes.

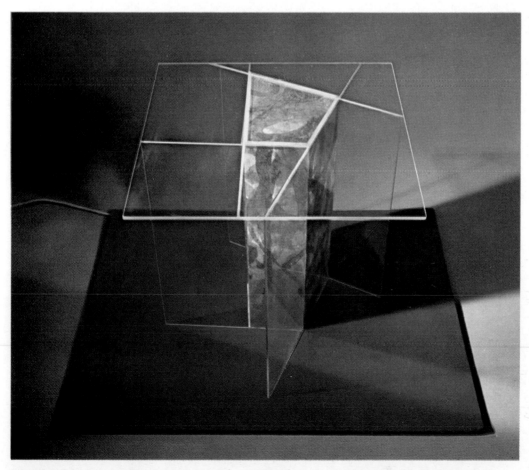

33. Plexiglass lamp-table. A dual-purpose, preplanned structure. (See also the illustration on page 135.)

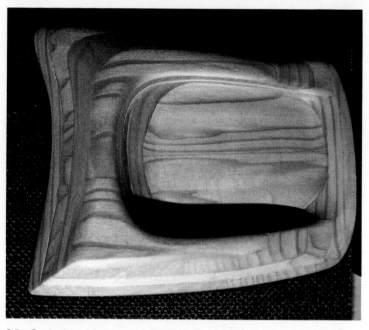

35. Cocktail server. Laminated plywood coated with varnish. The design was preplanned in pencil sketches. The two layers of plywood were fastened with waterproof emulsion glue and shaped by sensitive filing.

34. Wood experiment: additive and subtractive structure. Laminated surface overlays were fastened with glue and partially cut away by filing and sanding. Wedging and dowel rods were used for angular joining.

37. Wood box with cover. White pine with walnut. The unique quality of the design is a result of direct and intuitive carving of the material. The cover was subtly shaped and fitted, as no two sides are identical.

36. Cocktail server with glass. The design relates to the shape of the hand and things to be held.

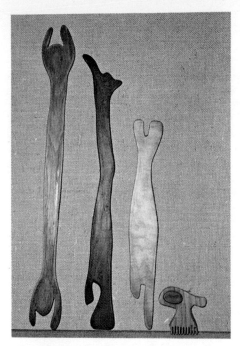

38. Shuttles and warp comb. The grain and pattern of the wood inspired the direct cutting and filing of these irregular shaped shuttles and comb.

39. Shuttles in use with the loom.

40. Wood toy by Joe Ordos. A kinetic structure in which the detachable joining of ears and tail allows for changes in position. Holes were drilled in the separate pieces to fit over projecting dowel rods.

41. Jigsaw puzzle. A structure of action made of silk-screened plywood painted with enamel. The design uses subjective animal motifs. (Courtesy: University of Wisconsin Arts Extension.)

42. Each unit of the jigsaw is an effective design when seen separately or as part of the whole puzzle. (Courtesy: University of Wisconsin Arts Extension.)

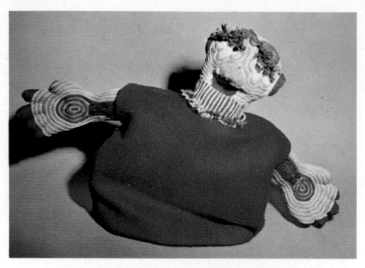

43. Puppet of rope and felt. Shapes and patterns of rope were fastened by invisible sewing through the strands. (Courtesy: Chicago Public Schools.)

44. Raffia container. Coil binding and double-knot stitch were used. The bird form was created by changes in contour, color, pattern and texture.

45. Rope-covered bottles. Examples of the diversity of patterns that can be created by the manipulation and wrapping of twisted paper rope.

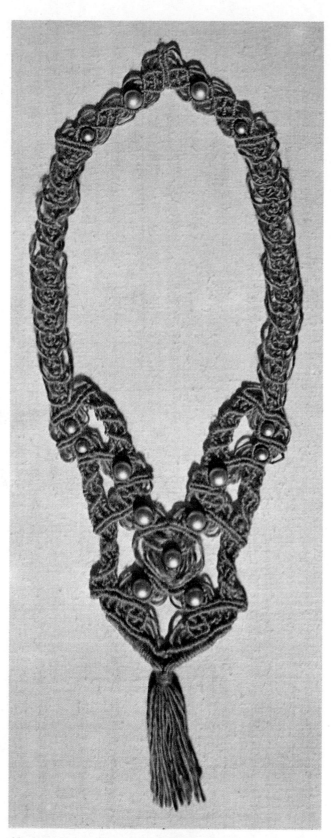

46. Macramé necklace by Joan Paque. Knotting of soft nylon cord was combined with wood beads.

CHAPTER 7/Crafts of Flexible Materials: Felt, Leather, Metal, Paper

Flexible materials are those which are pliable and capable of being modified and manipulated by hand. A comparative exploration of the "look" and "feel" of such materials as felt, leather, metal and paper reveals varying degrees of firmness and flexibility. The pliability of the material depends partly on the thickness and weight of the material as well as on the inherent texture, composition and method of fabrication. In spite of distinguishing differences between these materials, all of them have some common structural possibilities and require the use of similar tools and processes.

Working with the Materials

In the preceding chapter, a number of the processes which are directly applicable to crafts of flexible materials were described. The section on edge cutting with shears and knives is found on page 55.

To the general remarks on internal cutting found on page 57 may be added one or two suggestions. To cut away small shapes of flexible material, use a mat knife, safety-razor blade or chisel. To cut away large shapes, use these same tools to make slits along the design. Then, using these slits as a "starter," insert scissors or shears to complete the cutting more rapidly. Also, try making partial slits and cuts without removing any of the material. Lift the material at the cut to flex and bend it back, revealing the cut-out opening.

Two-Dimensional Structures of Flexible Materials

Internal cutting by means of perforating is discussed on page 57. Perforating is useful in creating two-dimensional structures that feature inlays. (See page 64.)

SURFACE OVERLAYS. Use contrasting colors, textures, and shapes of material for visual interest as well as structural support. Sewing and lacing are by far the most adaptive and versatile methods of attaching felt and leather overlays, as they retain the general flexibility of the materials. (See the diagrams on pages 105 and 107 for basic stitches.) Adhesives, staples, eyelets and office-type metal fasteners are effective for the fastening of papers and cardboards. Epoxy cement, rivets and soldering should be used for fastening metal overlays.

Three-Dimensional Structures of Soft Flexible Materials

GUSSET STRUCTURES. Gussets are used for the side walls of craft objects like bags, briefcases, portfolios and other containers that require depth and added space. They can be made by folding the edges of the material or by the addition of separate pieces of material. These pieces are usually cut into rectangular, triangular or curved shapes. Expandable gussets are made by folding and creasing the material before attaching it to the sides. Sewing and lacing are generally used for the fastening of felt and leather gussets. Adhesives are used for the attachment of paper gussets.

DART FORMATIONS. Tapered seams of V-shaped insertions can be used to change the contour of flat, flexible sheet material. These are commonly used for the fitting of garments, boots, sandals, gloves and other costume accessories.

STUFFED FORMS. Felt and leather are suitable for making three-dimensional soft structures. (See Color Plates 10, 13, 15, and 18.) Cut two identical pieces of the material of the desired shapes. Sew the edges together all around except for about six inches to allow for the insertion of the filler. Cotton batting, foam-rubber chips, and any other soft material can be used to fill and expand the form. After stuffing, sew the opening.

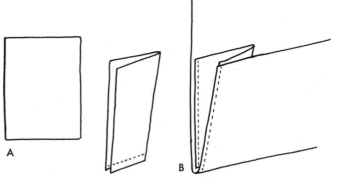

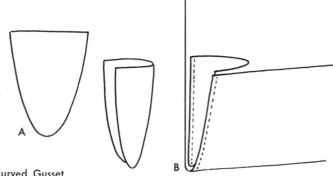

Rectangular Gusset
(A) Fold gusset lengthwise and stitch bottom edges together.
(B) Insert and attach to outer edges of material.

Curved Gusset
(A) Fold gusset lengthwise.
(B) Insert and attach by shaping outer edges of material to follow the curve of the gusset.

One-Piece Folded Gusset
(A) Cut material with extended sides to allow for depth of gusset.
(B) Reverse material inside-out and sew gusset edges together.
(C) Turn material to outer side. Pull gussets inward so that they can be covered when the flap is closed.

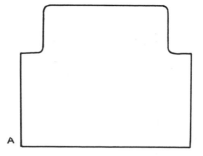

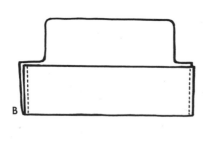

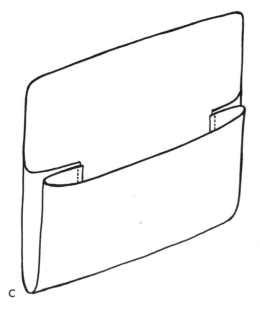

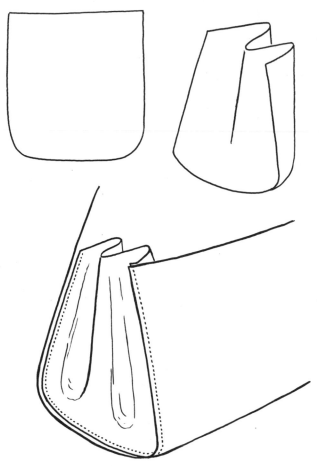

Expandable Gusset: Soft Fold
For soft, drapable felt and leathers.

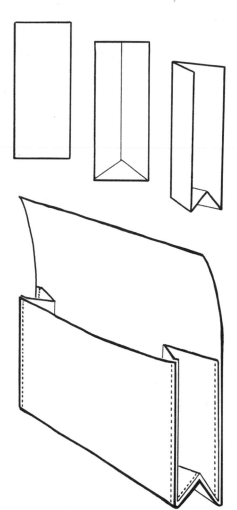

Expandable Gusset: Sharp Fold
For firm, thick felt and leathers.
Crease material into permanent pressed folds. Use steam iron to press felt. Use dampened leather to make sharply creased edges; allow to dry under pressure.

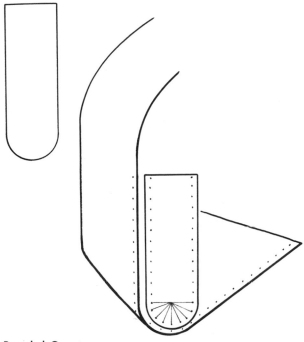

Rounded Gusset
Use identical spacing for the straight edges of the gusset and the outer edges of the material. Use radial spacing for the curved portion of the gusset.

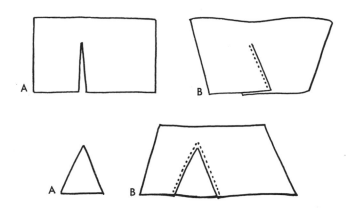

Single Darts
Single darts can be used for either thin or heavy weights of material.

Overlapping Darts
(A) Slit material with scissors or knife.
(B) Overlap material to reduce length of edge.

Inserted Darts
(A) Cut V-shaped piece of material.
(B) Insert material to expand edge.

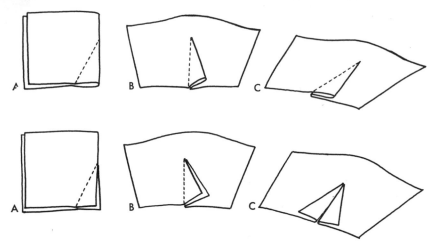

Double Darts
Double darts can only be used for thin weights of sheet material.

Uncut Double Darts
(A) Stitch material.
(B) Fold material to overlap one side.
(C) Flatten by pressing.

Slit Double Darts
(A) Stitch material.
(B) Slit edge.
(C) Open and spread at seam to distribute thickness.

Four-Dimensional Structures of Action and Motion

Flexible materials such as felt, leather, paper and cardboard, as well as metal, are readily adaptable for mobiles and other types of participative structures. Metal is commonly used because it has the additional appeal of producing tinkling or clanging sounds.

To make mobiles, use any of the cutting or manipulative processes to make either flat shapes or dimensional forms. Punch or drill holes in the material. Use wire or cord to suspend the pieces and allow for variable movements and arrangements. Mobile structures can be used to add interest to numerous kinds of household hangers, racks and lamps as well as to costume jewelry and toys.

Participative structures call for the involvement of the viewer to make changes in the position of shapes and forms. Puzzles, movable toys and dolls, as seen in Color Plates 10, 15, 18, 40, 41 and 42, are typical examples.

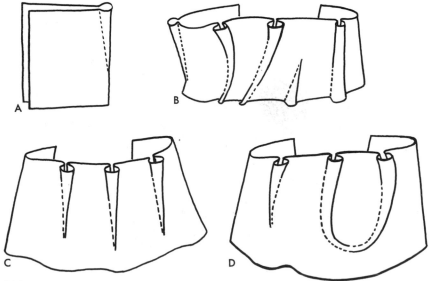

Rounded Darts
Rounded darts can be used for the fastening and shaping of flexible material into three-dimensional forms. They can be used to change the contour of the material and also to add to the decorative interest.
(A) Tapered dart.
(B) Curved edge darts.
(C) Symmetrical arrangement of tapered darts.
(D) Asymmetrical arrangement of curved darts.

100

FELT

Source and Method of Production

Felt is a fibrous material produced by the matting or felting together of wool and other fibers such as those derived from cotton, fur and numerous synthetic materials. Some wool must be used, as the felting process depends on the tendency of wool to coil, entangle and bond fibers together. The matted material is moistened and saturated with steam and then passed through oscillating and vibrating plates which tangle the fibers. Additional moisture and a soapy lubricant are applied with steam rollers to shrink and mat the fibers together to a firm finish. The material can be compressed and hardened to various degrees of flexibility.

Distinguishing Characteristics

The material is available in a much greater range of weights and thickness than any woven material. It can be processed from ½₂" to 3" thick. Its insulating and cushioning qualities are an asset for many purposes. Felt of average fabric weight is commonly used for craftmaking. Its chief advantage over fabric is that it does not unravel when it is cut. It can be dyed in any and all colors and made in various textures.

The following information and suggestions pertain specifically to felt and supplement the general instructions for cutting, fastening, manipulations and surface treatment given in the previous chapter. Examples of felt craft are illustrated in color, Plates 9 through 15.

Fastening Processes

PASTING AND GLUING. Use adhesives sparingly as they tend to discolor and stiffen the material. The spray-type dispensers make it easier to control the application of the adhesives on flexible weights of felt. Liquid types of adhesives should only be used to fasten thick blocks of the material.

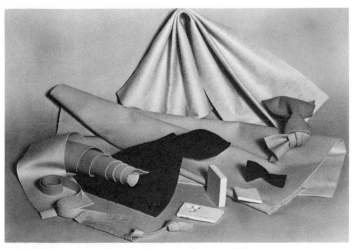

Felt of various weights, thicknesses and textural sheen.

Felt alligator toy. Experimental design. Experiments with cutting and fastening processes were featured as structural motifs.

METAL FASTENING. Fabric weights of felt are inclined to stretch. Therefore, it is important to punch holes slightly smaller to allow for the enlargement of the openings when they are to be used for eyelets, grommets, rapid rivets, and snap fasteners.

SEWING. Sewing is the most effective method for fastening fabric weights of felt. Both hand and machine sewing also add to the firmness and durability of the material. Use rows of stitches to reinforce any cut edges and prevent stretching. For inconspicious stitches, match the color of thread and sew only halfway through the material so that the stitches do not show on the surface.

Manipulative Processes

ROLLING. Rolling is one of the most exciting possibilities for the manipulation of felt. Since the edges do not unravel, it is a quick way to form the material with a minimum of fastening. Many types of cylindrical forms can be created. Cut several colors of felt into bands or ribbons; then, roll them together and fasten them with decorative stitches through the roll. Small rolls can be used for beads or buttons; large rolls can be used for toys and cushions.

SHIRRING. Shirring and gathering are other methods of manipulation that are peculiarly suitable for felt. Use perforations or eyelets along an edge; gather the material with cords or laces. Also try shirring the material into ruffled formations by using a needle with heavy button thread.

BLOCKING. Blocking is one of the most versatile and practical methods of manipulating felt. Steaming the material softens the matted fibers and makes it possible to stretch the felt into three-dimensional formations. This can be done by pushing and pulling with fingers or over a wooden form such as is used for the blocking of hats.

Felt tote bag. Spontaneous design. Machine stitching is used for fastening, stiffening and decorative design.

Puzzle Pillow. Stuffed felt; preplanned design. Preliminary sketches were made of different shapes and possibilities for fitting the parts together. An example of participative structure of active involvement. (See Color Plate 10.)

Leather of various weights and textures: fluffy sheepskin, crisp reptile, soft suede, smooth calf and firm cowhide.

LEATHER

Source and Method of Production

Leather is the hide or skin of an animal. The more common sources are the domestic animals: cattle, goat, sheep and pig. The rarer sources are the birds and reptiles: ostrich, alligator, lizard, and snake. (Hopefully, the craftsman will stand firmly against any use of skins from rare and protected species.)

Perishable skins are converted into durable leather by the tanning process. In vegetable tanning, the hides are soaked in tanning liquid, which is a strongly astringent substance obtained from bark such as sumac. The process involves several months. It is important to the craftsman, as only vegetable-tanned leathers can be used for stamping and tooling. Chemical or chrome tanning is the quickest method of tanning. The process can be done in a day. The chemicals, which are obtained from chromite, are used for both the preserving and coloring of hides. Chemically treated leather cannot be tooled because the fibers of the skin are permanently shrunk in the process and cannot be re-stretched by tooling. This is the reason that chrome-tanned leather is more resistant to scuffing and wear.

Distinguishing Characteristics

Since leather is a natural material, its surface texture is variable, depending on the animal source and process of production. It may be pliant, soft and drapable or firmly flexible or even stiff and rigid. For leathercraft examples in color, see Plates 16 through 21.

The "top grain" of leather is the outer, or hair, side of the hide and is much more durable than the skin. The top grain can easily be detected by the pores of the skin. It usually has a smooth, subtle, soft, dull sheen. Split-grain leathers are artificially grained, glazed, and coated and have a much more uniform machine-made texture than top-grain leathers. The coatings make them stiff and glossy, and they are inclined to chip, peel and crack when folded or creased.

Suede leathers, which are also made from the underside of the skin, are not coated. They are soft and flexible but much more fragile than coated leathers. Soft garment leathers, which are similar to suede, are lightly coated with a flexible waterproof finish. They are washable and much more durable than suede.

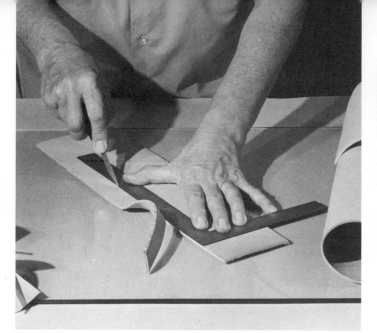

Cutting leather. A blade is used along a metal ruler over plate glass.

Skiving leather is the thinning of edges to be fastened.

Cutting Processes

CUTTING ON GLASS. To cut firm leather, place it on a piece of plate glass and use a mat knife or razor blade along a metal-edged ruler. Sole leather can be cut with a coping saw if it is too thick to be cut with a knife or razor blade.

SKIVING. Skiving is a means of thinning leather edges by cutting away layers from the underside of the skin. Any edges that are to be turned under should be skived to relieve the bulk and thickness and facilitate creasing and fastening. Place the leather on a hard surface; hold the knife almost flat to prevent cutting through the skin. Remove thin layers, one at a time, until the edge can be folded easily. A ready-made holder for ejector-razor blades can be used to expedite the process.

Fastening Processes

SEWING. Thin leathers such as suede and garment leathers can be sewn easily with ordinary needles and thread. Heavier leathers require preliminary punching or pricking. Use an awl or any pointed tool to punch the holes. For machine sewing thin leathers, use the same techniques and same kind of needle and thread used for the general sewing of fabrics. Household sewing machines can also be used to sew heavy leathers by replacing the standard needle with a heavy-duty needle.

SADDLE STITCHING. Saddle stitching is one of the quickest and most effective ways to fasten two or more pieces of firm leathers. It is also a means of reinforcing single edges of leather to prevent uneven stretching. Use a thonging chisel to cut slits and mark uniform spacing. Decide on the size of the thonging chisel to be used before cutting the final pieces of leather so that the spacing can be planned to come out evenly at the corners and turns. Two blunt-point needles are needed.

Suede leather belt. Hand sewing and shirring of edges is used as a structural design motif.

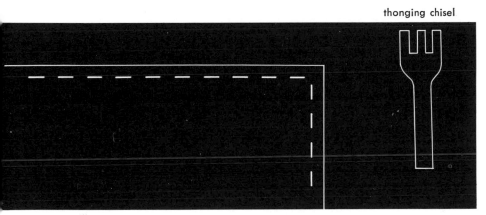

thonging chisel

Saddle Stitching
Use thonging chisel to cut slits of uniform length and spacing.

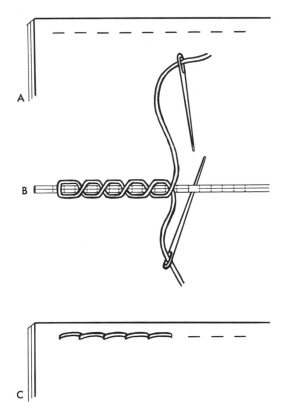

Saddle Stitching
(A) Top view. Slits made with thonging chisel.
(B) Sectional side view. Two needles threaded with one piece of thread alternately pass through each slit two times: first, from the bottom up; then, from top down.
(C) Top view with portion of completed stitches.

Use a heavy button thread or waxed thread made especially for saddle stitching. Thread one needle at each end of the thread. Alternately sew through each slit in the leather two times: first use one needle from the top down; then, use the other needle through the same slit from the bottom up. (See diagrams.) Pull the stitches tight but avoid shirring or puckering.

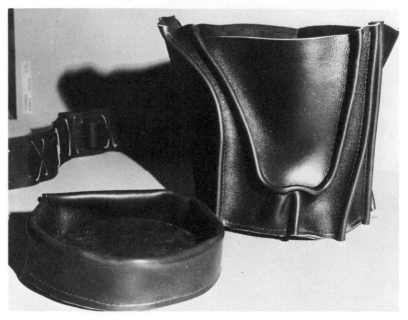

Leather manipulation and fastening. Structural design motif. Saddle stitching was used to fasten and reinforce edges.

LEATHER LACING. Goat and calf skins are generally used for the manufacture of leather lacing. Lacing is most commonly made in ⅛″ or narrower widths. However, a thin weight of Florentine lacing is usually made in widths from ¼″ to ½″. Lacing is most suitable for fastening the kinds of leathers that are too heavy for hand stitching or machine sewing.

The diagrams show three kinds of stitches that are adaptable to many variations: the running stitch, the whipped-edge stitch and the layover stitch. Regardless of which stitch is used, the results will be more effective if the work is done with rhythmic continuity and speed. For accurate measurement of holes, use a spacing wheel along a ruler; then, punch the holes a shade larger than the width of the lacing. For slits, which are less conspicuous than holes, use a thonging chisel. This simultaneously marks the spacing and cuts the slits. Leather-lacing needles expedite the insertion of the lacing through the holes and slits. However, lacing can be done without a needle if the lacing is firm and is cut to a tapered point or is stiffened with a drop of nail polish.

It is important to pull the lacing tight enough to bind the edge but avoid puckering; the laced edges should lie flat. After the lacing is completed, the entire piece can be dampened and then the edges can be further flattened by pounding with a rubber mallet. Before pounding, protect the surface of the leather with a smooth piece of heavy paper like that used for file folders.

Do not begin or end the lacing at a corner or at a turn, because this is the most conspicuous and vulnerable part of the structure. It is easier to conceal the ends of the lacing along an edge. Cut the end to a tapered point and then insert it under the laced edge for about an inch of the distance to hold it securely. (See diagrams.)

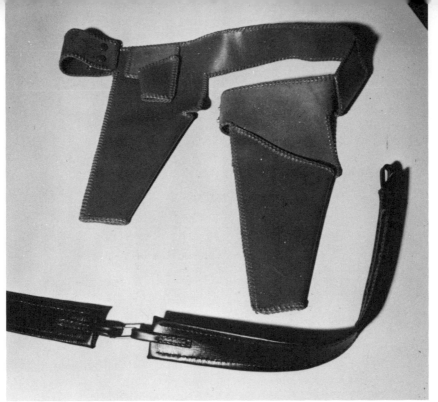

Boy's holster and belt fastened with leather lacing (layover stitch);
man's belt fastened with saddle stitching.

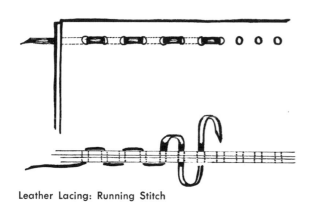

Leather Lacing: Running Stitch

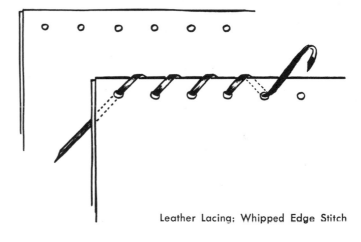

Leather Lacing: Whipped Edge Stitch

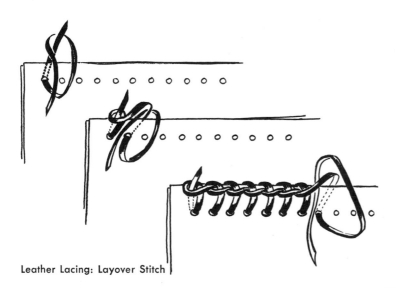

Leather Lacing: Layover Stitch

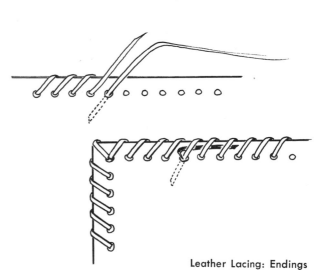

Leather Lacing: Endings

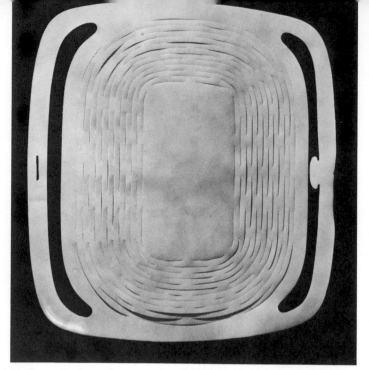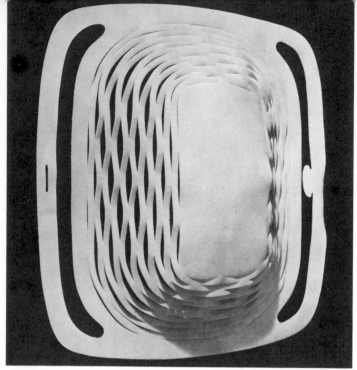

Leather tote bag. An example of functional and decorative use of internal cutting and manipulation. The two-dimensional sheet is cut and then manipulated to open up the sheet into the three-dimensional form.

Decorative Processes

STAMPING. Stamping tools are made in many different shapes and patterns. Simple geometric shapes are more adaptive for creative arrangements.

Only vegetable-tanned tooling leathers can be used for stamping. The thicker the tooling leather, the deeper the impressions attainable. Dampen the leather with a cloth or sponge from the back, or flesh,

Stamping leather.

Tooling leather.

side. To avoid spotting with water stains, always dampen the entire piece of leather, even if only a small part of it is to be stamped. If moisture oozes out under pressure, the leather is too wet and should be wiped off with a dry cloth and allowed to dry until it is just limp.

Lay the damp leather on a smooth surface such as a piece of Masonite or other wallboard. Pound the stamping tool with a hammer to make impressions in the leather. Avoid cutting through the top surface of the leather.

TOOLING. Place the dampened leather on a piece of plate glass, marble or any hard, smooth surface. Sketch the design on layout paper and then fasten the design over the leather with masking tape. Trace over the design with a hard, sharp pencil to make the impression on the leather. Remove the paper pattern. Use modeling tools to develop the design. If these are not available, orangewood sticks which are shaped for manicuring are a good, inexpensive substitute. Nutpicks and salvaged dental tools can also be used.

Linear tooling is the first step for all types of tooling. For deep, durable impressions, retrace the design over and over again.

For relief modeling, follow the same procedure as for linear tooling. Then, use modeling tools with a broad base to force the shapes and masses into relief by pressing down either the background or the pattern. Start with outlines of the designs and work away from them. Use a rotary movement and work over the entire design to be tooled before completing any one section or part. This is necessary to prevent stretching the piece out of shape. Work round and round with considerable pressure but take care to avoid creasing the leather.

For higher relief, trace the design on both the front and back sides of the leather. Then, alternately model first on the front side then on the back side. Use the linear tool to sharpen the edges.

COLORING AND FINISHING. Use leather dyes for brilliant coloring; use colored shoe polishes and colored dressings for more subtle tones. The colors of dyes and polishes penetrate the pores of the leather only if any previous dressing and coatings are removed with a dry-cleaning fluid. Otherwise, the color remains suspended on the surface and tends to rub off with wear.

Saddle soap is an ideal type of general cleaner for smooth-surfaced leathers, as it simultaneously cleans and restores the natural oils.

Two views of a clutch bag. Suede leather; preplanned design. The shapes and structural form were carefully considered in a series of preliminary sketches. The thoughtful planning makes allowance for changes of shape and form as the bag is either filled or emptied.

Black leather case. North European, 16th Century. Tooled leather. (Courtesy: The Metropolitan Museum of Art. Gift of Adele O. Friedman, through Harry G. Friedman, 1951.)

Leather belt and buckle. Spontaneous design. The fragments of various sizes and textures of leather were arranged spontaneously and fastened with saddle stitching as a structural motif for decoration.

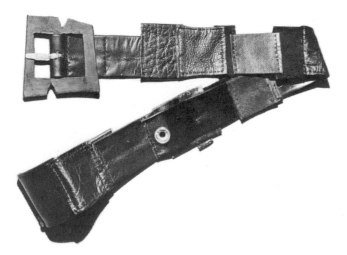

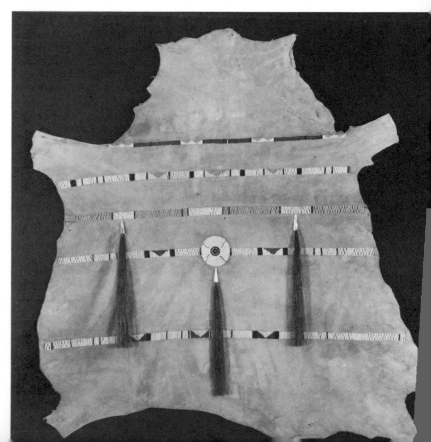

Leather skin robe. Geometric motifs with mobile horsehair pendants. Embroidered and decorated trim by Charles White, Sioux and Winnebago. (Courtesy: Institute of American Indian Arts, Santa Fe, New Mexico. Photo: Kay Wiest.)

Metal of different gauges and forms.

METAL

Source and Method of Production

Metal is an inorganic mineral substance. After extraction from ores, it is smelted into a molten state and then cast or extruded into solids, sheets, rods and wire. It is processed in varying degrees of hardness or temper by rolling or pounding. The temper that ranges from half-hard to spring-hard is used for pins, tongs and other sturdy fasteners that do not require soldering. The softer grades of metal, which can be soldered, are the most adaptive for craft projects. The thickness of metal is measured by gauge; the higher the number, the thinner the metal: 16 to 30 gauge is most versatile for hand crafts.

The pure elemental metals such as aluminum, copper, gold, silver, tin, iron and lead are usually combined or alloyed with other metals and chemical compounds to change color, malleability, hardness and durability. Brass, bronze, nickel silver and pewter are examples of alloy metals frequently used for crafts.

Distinguishing Characteristics

Metal is lustrous, malleable and fusible. It expands and contracts with temperature changes and is a conductor of heat and electricity. It is unusually strong for its weight. Nails, screws, bolts and countless other types of fasteners are predominately made of metal because of this high ratio of strength to size.

The color range of most metals is of the subtle grayish tones; the more intense colors are the warm yellows of gold and brass and the reddish tones of copper or the blue-greens of patinaed bronze.

The following instructions for the cutting, fastening, manipulation and surface treatment of metal supplement the general instructions given in Chapter 6.

Fastening Processes

RIVETING. Riveting is a strong and permanent method of joining metals. Ready-made rivets are available in various diameters, sizes and types: tubular, solid and split-shaft. Rivets can also be cut from wire of various metals. Drill or punch holes through the two pieces of metal to be joined. The holes should be slightly larger than the diameter of the rivet to be used. Align the holes. Place the shank of the rivet on a small anvil. Hammer the end of the rivet until it flattens out.

111

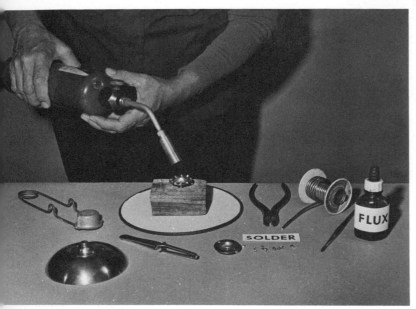

Soldering metal.

Structural forming process.

SOLDERING. Because of the fusibility of metal, soldering is one of the most effective ways to join most metals. The process involves the melting of soft, fusible alloys that melt at a lower temperature than the metals to be joined. The following steps are important: cleaning, choosing the solder, fluxing, heating and pickling.

Cleaning of the surfaces to be soldered is necessary. Most soldering failures are due to poor cleaning. Any paint, rust, oil, or grease, and even perspiration from the fingers, must be removed from the metals in the area where attachment is to be made. Use abrasives, scouring pads, steel wool or scraping to thoroughly clean the metals before attempting to solder.

Choosing the proper solder for the metals to be joined is important. Solders are produced in varying degrees of hardness to melt at different degrees of temperature. Soft solders, predominately of lead, melt at low temperatures and are used for soft metals such as tin and copper. Hard solders are alloys of the metal to be joined, combined with other, quick-fusing metals such as zinc and lead. These are available in sheets, rods or wire and can be cut into minute particles for very small and precise joining.

Fluxing is a step in the soldering process. Soldering flux is an acid preparation necessary to destroy the oxidization which occurs on most metals. Flux also promotes the flow of the solder. Borax powder is commonly used as a flux. Flux is also available in liquid or paste form. Apply flux to all of the surfaces of the metal to be joined, as well as to the solder. For small work, cut minute pellets of solder about 1/16" square. Immerse these in flux and then apply them to the metal with tweezers or a small brush.

Heating melts the solder. Electric soldering irons can be used for soft soldering. They are quick and convenient for many craft projects but are not suitable for hard solder or small, refined work. Torches which are designed to combine compressed air with gas are much more versatile. Beginners will find the propane canister torches very effective and adequate.

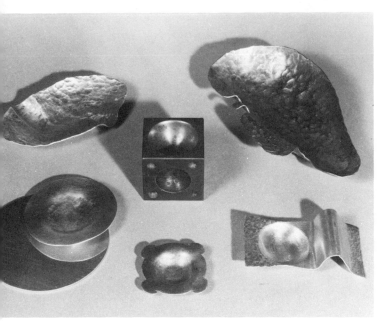

Structural forming; examples of experiments.

Aluminum bowl. Edge cutting and one-piece structural forming.

Place the metals on a charcoal block so that the metal will retain the heat. Protect the bench or worktable with a piece of asbestos. Apply heat by playing the flame over all surfaces of the metals until the flux appears whitish in color; then quickly direct the flame to the specific solder area until the bright flow of the melted solder appears at the joint. Allow the work to cool gradually or immerse it while still hot in a "pickling" solution, which simultaneously cleans and cools the metal.

Pickling is the last step. To remove the oxides that result from the heating processes such as annealing and soldering, make a solution of one part of sulfuric acid and ten parts of water; add the acid to the water. Use a pyrex tray. Heat the solution to speed up the cleaning process. To immerse the object, use wood or nickel tongs—not iron or steel, as they affect the solution. Rinse thoroughly in running water.

Manipulative Processes

BENDING. Bending is the quickest way to create three-dimensional structures of one piece of material, as the metal retains its position without any additional support. Most metals of 16 to 20 gauge can be bent into curved or angular shapes by hand. To bend heavier and harder metals, place the material over a wood edge or vise; then, pound it with a mallet.

FORMING AND STRETCHING. Metal can be stretched and shaped into a diversity of hollow forms by alternately hammering and annealing. Since most metals become hard and brittle when they are hammered, they must be annealed to prevent cracking. Annealing is the process of softening metal by heating it to a dull-red heat. Use an electric stove, gas flame or torch to heat the entire piece evenly. Aluminum should only be heated to a dull pink color. Pewter is malleable without any annealing, as it is an exceptionally soft metal.

113

The depth of the form is obtained by stretching the metal through continued hammering over a hollowed piece of hard wood or a depression in a sturdy canvas sandbag. Begin to hammer from the center of the metal to the outside, rotating the metal while doing this. For a smooth surface, use a wood or rawhide mallet. For a textured surface, use a ball peen or chasing hammer. Hammer blows must be even and close together. The form is deepened by repeated annealing and successive cleaning and hammering. When the edges begin to curl and wave, place the edge upside down on a flat, wood block or metal stake or anvil; then, smooth or "planish" it with a wood mallet. Trim irregular edges with shears or a saw. Use needle files to file the rough edges to a smooth, rounded finish.

Surface Treatment

COLORING. Chemical color changes can be achieved with specially prepared mordants which contain sulfur compounds. The chemicals used vary, depending on the metals to be used. Immerse the metal in the coloring solution or apply it with a brush. Interesting contrasts can be achieved by removing the coloring from some areas with a fine abrasive. To preserve the color, apply a coating of clear lacquer.

Experiments with surface treatment.

Pair of funerary sandals. Egyptian, 1501–1447 B.C. Heavy sheet gold. An example of cutting, fastening, manipulation and surface treatment. (Courtesy: The Metropolitan Museum of Art. Fletcher Fund, 1926.)

Silver bowl with anthropomorphic design. An example of forming and repoussé surface treatment. (Courtesy: The Museum of Primitive Art, New York.)

114

TAPPING OR CHASING. Any pointed tools can be used on thin metals over 24 gauge for tapping and chasing. Extremely thin metals over 36 gauge are so impressionable that they can be tapped without a hammer. For heavier metals, strike the tool with a hammer to make the impression. This process differs from piercing and perforating in that the tool merely indents the metal. Special steel chasing tools are needed for metals from 24 to 16 gauge. To prevent warping, it is best to outline the entire design first. Then, tap down either the background or the pattern. At first, tap the markings about ¼″ apart all over the area to be tapped. Then, tap more closely until the pattern stands out in relief.

REPOUSSÉ. Repoussé is the process of stretching thin metals to create relief patterns. Use thin metals of 34 to 38 gauge. Work on a smooth linoleum surface or on a padding of newspapers. First, outline the design with a pencil and indent the outline with a pointed modeling tool. Then, turn the metal over and use a rotary motion with a broad modeling tool to press down on areas within the outline so that the design stands out in relief on the opposite side. A wood dowel rod makes a good repoussé tool as it can be cut to the length of a pencil and then shaped to any type of point with a knife.

Finishing

CLEANING AND ASHING. Wash metal in an ammonia solution or a detergent. Then, follow by ashing with abrasives such as powdered pumice or kitchen cleansers. Use course abrasives first to wear down the metal surface to eliminate scratches. Follow with successive applications of finer abrasives.

POLISHING AND COATING. Numerous polishing and buffing compounds are available. Polish with a soft cloth dipped in rouge powder or rouge paste or use patented metal polishes according to the directions given. For a high luster, buff the metal with felt or chamois. To preserve the finish and prevent tarnishing, paint or spray the metal with a clear lacquer.

(Right) Brooch of cast silver by Michael Jerry.

(Below) Silver pin by Michael Jerry. Spontaneous design evolved through manipulation of the metal. The resulting shapes suggested the setting of the stone as an accent.

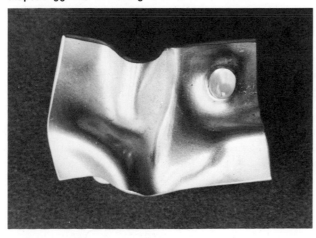

PAPER

Source and Method of Production

Paper is made from decomposed rags, straw, bark, wood or other fibrous material. The material is reduced to a pulp by beating, grinding and floating on water which is kept in motion to distribute the fibers evenly. When the natural structure of the fibrous substance is broken down, the filaments mat easily. The surface of the water is thus coated with a thin film or tissue of cellulose derived from plant structure. The water is drained off through wire meshes and the sheets are then laid out on an absorbent substance such as felt. The layers of paper are alternated with felt and then pressed to squeeze out the remaining water. The sheets are dried and finished by sizing with glue or gelatin and smoothed by means of pressure.

Distinguishing Characteristics

The material is generally made in flexible sheets but it is also produced in stiff and rigid weights in the form of cardboards and wallboards. Its strength and durability depend on its fabrication. It may be extremely fragile or tough and durable. The color range is unlimited. It can be processed in a diverse range of textures: smooth, rough, dull, shiny, transparent, opaque, soft, brittle, absorbent, nubby, pebbly, fibrous or patterned. Paper is also used as a base for numerous kinds of coatings such as wax, sand, tar and metals. Chemically treated papers include the light-sensitive photographic and blueprint papers.

All of the basic methods of cutting, fastening, manipulation and surface treatment can be used for structuring crafts of paper. The illustrative examples show that paper is an especially suitable material for the various manipulative processes.

The following pages cover paper sculpture and five methods of converting paper into papier-mâché, which is one of the most versatile ways of structuring craft objects from paper.

Paper: diversity in textures, colors and forms of a commonplace material.

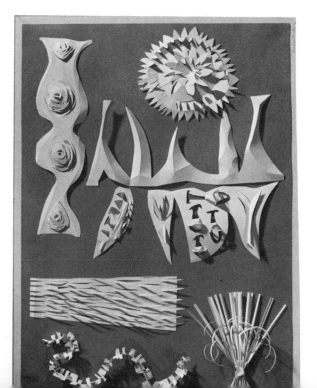

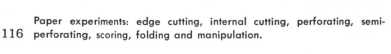

Paper experiments: edge cutting, internal cutting, perforating, semi-perforating, scoring, folding and manipulation.

Paper Knight on Paper Horse. Preplanned design. After several experiments with preliminary structures the final design was created from only one piece of paper. The one-piece structure was achieved by edge cutting, internal cutting and scoring and pull-outs from within the piece of paper. Slits and slots were used for fastening; no adhesives were needed.

Paper Sculpture

One-piece paper structures are the most durable kind of paper sculpture as they are self-supporting and do not require any adhesives or additional fastening materials. Any medium-weight, flexible paper can be used.

CUTTING. Avoid cutting away any part of the piece of paper. More strength and dimension result from cutting into the edges or making cuts within the piece of paper before manipulating it.

SCORING AND BENDING. Scoring is the most essential process for paper sculpture. Use a knife or razor blade to cut only partway through the thickness of the paper; then, gently coax and fold the paper away from the cut surface. Experiment with the particular paper at hand to determine the exact amount of pressure needed. The flat sheet of paper can be manipulated into three-dimensional formations by alternately scoring and bending: first, on one side; then, on the reverse side. Try straight, diagonal, and curved lines as well as combinations.

SEMI-PERFORATING. Use hollow drive punches for circular cuts, and chisels or a knife or razor blade for squared shapes. Cut through the paper for only one-half of the shape so that the paper can be pulled out and folded back. This reveals both the positive and negative areas of the form and accentuates light and shadow.

EDGE CUTTING AND FRINGING. Use scissors to make a series of closely spaced cuts into the edges of the paper. Curl or bend the cut edge to emphasize the form.

FOLD CUTTING. Score and fold the paper; then, make two separate cuts into it at a right angle to the fold. Then, pull the shape out in the opposite direction.

SLOTTING AND FASTENING. Use a knife or blade to cut a slit or slot within the piece of paper; then, pull one corner or a projecting shape through the slot to interlock the shapes.

Papier-Mâché

Papier-mâché is closely related to the initial source and method of producing paper. It involves the decomposition of paper by tearing it into small pieces or strips and soaking it in water until it can be "mashed" or modeled and manipulated. The term is also generally applied to any types of crafts made from salvaged papers and paper products. (See Color Plates 22 through 26.)

MAKING PAPIER-MÂCHÉ

PAPER PULP METHOD. Tear newspaper into small bits about the size of confetti. Make the pieces as small and ragged as possible. Avoid glossy or hard-surfaced newspapers as these take a much longer time to decompose. For a very fine pulp, use paper tissue or paper napkins. Put the torn paper in a jar and add enough water to soak it thoroughly. Overnight soaking is usually sufficient; longer soaking makes the pulp softer. Add about a tablespoon of salt to each quart of the mixture to prevent spoilage.

Grind the mixture into a pulp by rubbing it against the wire mesh of a strainer or by mashing it with a wooden spoon or stick. An electric food beater or paint mixer speeds up the grinding process. Drain off the surplus water, and the pulp is ready for use.

To use the pulp for a modeling medium, add just enough dry wallpaper, or similar, paste to make the mixture sticky. The soft pulp can be kept in a covered jar for several months provided it is not mixed with any paste in advance.

The pulp can be modeled into flat forms of low relief or used for solid three-dimensional formations. To create forms of larger scale, model the material over a wire-screen foundation. One of the chief assets of papier-mâché is that it can easily be combined with other materials without any special attachments. The mixture of paste or glue with the pulp adheres to all types of materials: glass beads, colored stones, seashells; wire and metal. These kinds of materials can be embedded in the pulp during the modeling process, and they become an integral part of the structure.

After modeling, place the piece on wax paper to dry. After the pulp is thoroughly dried, it can be sandpapered if a smooth finish is desired. It can be drilled to make holes for lacing pieces together as may be needed for necklaces (Color Plates 24 and 25.), belts and other craft purposes.

PAPER STRIP METHOD. This method is chiefly used to make hollow forms like those needed for face masks and other types of pageantry. It is also used for stage properties, as it is a quick way to create structures of large scale.

To get acquainted with the process, it is a good idea to start with a small foundation form such as a plastic bowl, a metal can or a balloon. Oil-based modeling clay such as plasticene makes a good foundation for face masks if refined features are desired.

Apply a thin coat of oil, vaseline or cold cream to the foundation. Lay cheesecloth or gauze over the oiled form; this can easily be pushed and stretched around to fit the form.

Tear some newspaper into uneven strips of about one-inch or two-

Making papier-mâché: paper pulp method.

Paper pulp experiments: modeling, embedding and surface treatment.

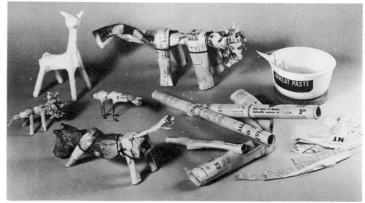

Japanese toy doll. Papier-mâché; paper pulp of Japanese rice paper. (Collection: Elizabeth Stein.)

Making papier-mâché: paper strip method. Two types of foundations for hollow form structures: oil clay and balloons.

Making papier-mâché: box and tube method.

Making papier-mâché: rolled paper method.

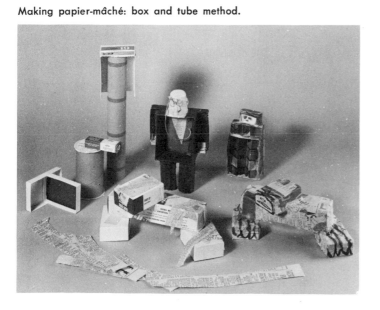

inch width; soak these strips in a liquid mixture of water and wallpaper paste until they flex easily. Remove one strip at a time and apply it over the cheesecloth; overlap and crisscross the strips to cover the entire form with one layer. Allow the layer to dry slightly before adding each successive one. Three to four layers of newspaper are usually adequate for a hull of about ¹⁄₁₆″ thickness. When the hull is dry, remove the foundation form. The structure is ready for paint or any other type of surface treatment.

ROLLED PAPER METHOD. Make about five or six rolls of newspaper of various lengths and diameters. Use only two or three sheets of paper for each roll so that they are not too firm to manipulate. Use masking tape to fasten each roll in several places. Bend and twist the rolls to express the form of a subject: animals, birds or people. Tie the rolls together with string to hold the parts together loosely. This makes it possible to adjust the action of the subject before the final fastening. Small pieces of gummed tape or strips of newspaper soaked in wallpaper paste can be used for the final fastening of the rolls. Even after the structure is joined, it can still be manipulated to make changes in position until the paste is thoroughly dried. To make the form smooth, use the paper strip method to pad the irregularities.

BOX AND TUBE METHOD. Select three or four paper boxes or cartons such as containers from salt, cereal and medicines. Choose a variety of shapes and forms: square, rectangular and tubular. Play with arrangements of these until they suggest a subject. Attach the boxes and tubes together with staples or paper fasteners or gummed tape. Try to utilize the form of the cartons as a vital part of the idea as well as the structure. Using the box and tube structure as an armature, add paper pulp, paper strips or draped paper to refine the form.

DRAPED PAPER METHOD. Use any medium-weight paper—preferably with an absorbent texture. Soak the entire sheet of paper in a liquid mixture of wallpaper paste. Square or rectangular baking dishes make an excellent container for papers up to 12″ x 18″. The paper can be folded over several times but should be moved around while it is soaking. Soak it until it is limp and pliable. The exact amount of time depends on the weight and texture of the paper. Drape and manipulate the paper into folds and twists. Heavier papers will remain rigid enough to be self-supporting. If additional support is needed, rolls of dried newspapers or other materials such as screen wire or wire hangers can be used.

FINISHING

All types of coloring and coating mediums can be used for the finishing of craft objects made of papier-mâché. Acrylic paints are especially suitable as they dry quickly and also add strength to the structure because of their binding medium. Some of the most effective results are achieved when the coloring and finishing mediums are used with restraint to avoid concealing the original texture of the papier-mâché.

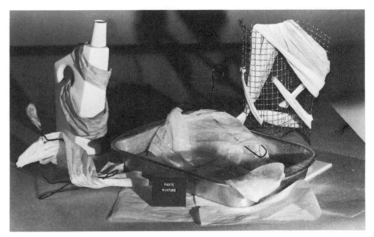

Making papier-mâché: draped paper method.

(Left) *Bikini on the Beach.* Papier-mâché. Paper pulp combined with box and strip structure; painted with acrylics.

(Below) *Bouncing Man off Horse.* Papier-mâché using rolled paper method.

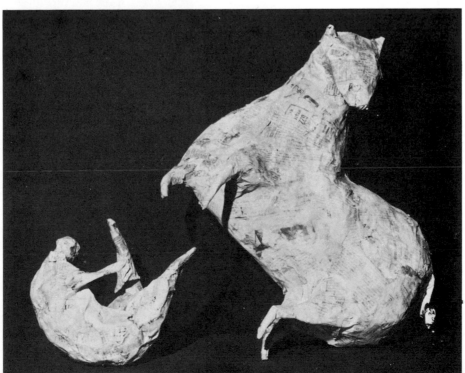

Cork bark and sheets of composition cork.

Various textures and forms of cork.

CHAPTER 8/Crafts of Rigid Materials: Cork, Plastic, Wood

Rigid materials are generally firm, stiff and solid. They are characterized by an unyielding inflexibility. The variations in grain, texture and porosity depend on their source and method of composition and fabrication. While firmness and rigidity are the dominant qualities of these materials, the photographs show that each of them can also be processed in flexible sheets and linear forms. The following instructions and suggestions for experimentation deal primarily with the rigid forms of these materials.

Working with the Materials

For the most part, processes for working with the rigid materials have been covered in Chapter 6. In cutting subtractive structures of one piece of material, sawing and filing (pages 54 to 56) are suggested for edge cutting. For internal cutting, drilling (page 57) and internal sawing (page 58) are described. The embellishment of the surface by cutting may be accomplished by means of incising. (See page 58.)

Relief carving goes a step beyond incising in that the design is first incised on the surface, and then parts are cut away. (See page 60.) Three-dimensional carving, most readily associated with working with wood, can be done in cork and plastic as well. A brief description of the carving process is found on page 60. The rigid materials lend themselves well to four-dimensional carving, a challenging approach to form. See page 60 for a description and summary of the process.

In creating additive structures of two or more pieces, several approaches are possible. All involve shaping of the materials and joining or fastening them in one way or another. Surface overlays, a type of laminating, will produce a structure of relatively low relief. (See page 62.) In working with the rigid materials, use adhesives, metal fasteners or lacing to attach the overlay pieces together. Surface inlays are discussed on page 64. The decorative pattern or design made of inlaid woods is known as intarsia. In one approach to a more three-dimensional additive form, the pieces of rigid materials can be so joined as to allow spaces between, producing an open, layered structure. This is described in the passage on surface projection, page 65.

As pointed out in Chapter 6, the most widely used method of fastening the rigid materials into a firm structure is angular joining, discussed on page 65. Although associated primarily with woodworking, it is also useful for joining the other rigid materials.

In creating structures out of the rigid materials, the possibilities of structures of action and motion should not be overlooked. The rigid materials lend themselves particularly well to the creation of mobiles and kinetic forms (page 66).

CORK

Source and Method of Production

Cork is a natural material stripped from the outer bark of the cork oak tree. It is chiefly a product of the Mediterranean area and commonly used for floats, buoys, bottle stoppers, insulation and gaskets. Composition cork is made from the waste cuttings of these natural cork products. The waste is ground up into either fine or coarse granules and then compressed into sheets or solid forms.

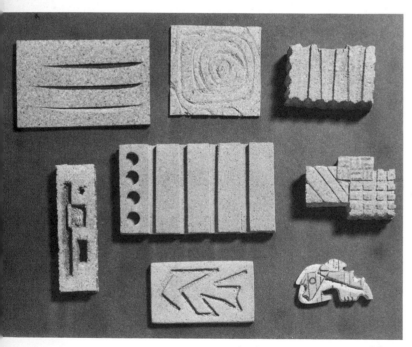

Cork experiments: cutting possibilities.

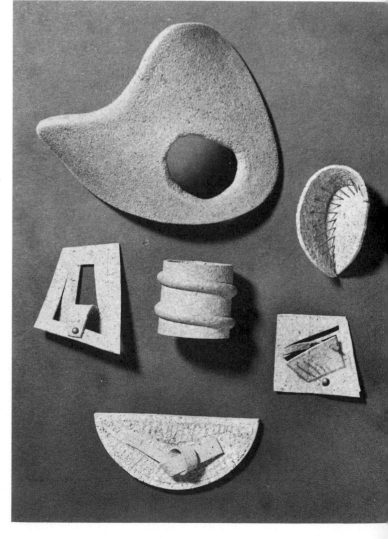

Cork experiments: manipulative possibilities.

Cork experiments: fastening possibilities.

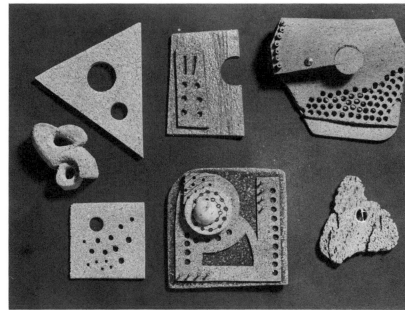

Cork experiments: decorative possibilities.

Cork experiments: fastening possibilities.

Distinguishing Characteristics

Cork possesses a combination of unique properties which peculiarly fit it for many uses for which it alone is suitable. It is light in weight, buoyant in water, and resilient to compressive stresses. Tough and durable, it withstands extremes in weather changes. The natural cork bark, which is tougher and more durable than the composition cork, is usually one to two inches thick and has an irregular grain and woody texture. Composition cork, which has the advantage of availability in any size, shape, form and thickness, has a uniform, granular texture. Thin sheets are very fragile and inclined to tear unless they are backed up with paper or cloth. Sheets over ⅛″ in thickness are much more durable and versatile. Solid blocks of fine granule composition cork that are one to two inches thick are as durable as natural cork. However, thick blocks of chunky coarse granules are inclined to chip and break apart unless attached to a firm ground.

The illustrations show how the basic tools and processes for structuring materials relate to the use of cork. The examples of experiments with the cutting, fastening, manipulation and surface treatment of the material reveal its many structural and decorative possibilities. The finished craft objects show the versatility of the material for many different uses.

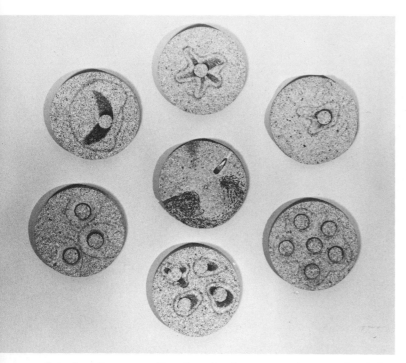

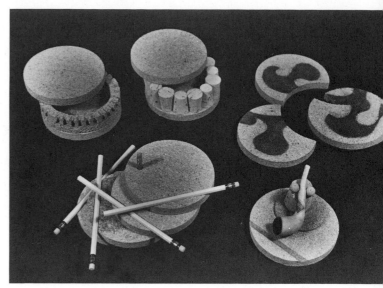

Various crafts of cork disks. A spontaneous response to the same material suggests different uses to different people.

Set of cork coasters. Two-dimensional structures. Spontaneous design. Each coaster is related to the others in size, material and technique, but no two are alike because of the spontaneous variations in surface treatment.

Cork carvings. Identical blocks of cork carved by two different people show individuality in technique and style.

Sculptural view of trivet on pedestal and the same trivet in use.

Cork boxes. Additive structures. The spontaneous design for objects of the same size and purpose reveals striking differences in style and technique.

Cork cigarette holder. Subtractive one-piece structure. Spontaneous design.

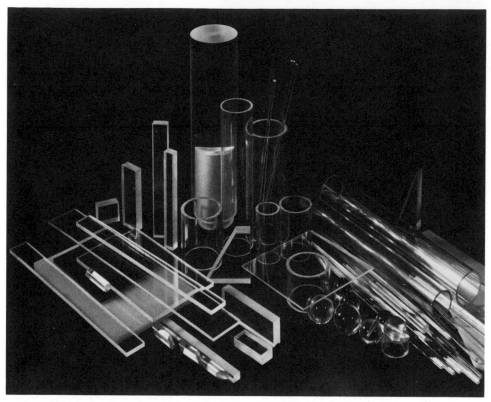

Various thicknesses and forms of clear plastic.

PLASTIC

Source and Method of Production

Plastics are synthetic materials made by means of chemistry. The term is applied in industry to those materials which are in a plastic state during manufacture. Various elements and substances such as cellulose, phenol, and formaldehyde are extracted from such natural sources as coal, wood and petroleum. These are put together and cooked until they lose their original identity and become an entirely new resinous material of honey-like consistency. The exact kind and proportion of each ingredient and the methods of manufacture vary according to the chemicals used and the ultimate use of the products. To make colored plastics, dyes are added to this honey-like mixture. For mottled or variegated colors, the dyes are only partially mixed. The manufacturing process is completed by casting, forming, molding or spinning.

Although there are hundreds of commercial trade names for plastics, most of the material can be classified broadly as either thermoplastic or thermosetting. The thermoplastic types can be softened and resoftened indefinitely by the application of heat and pressure. They can easily be formed at the moderate temperatures attainable in an ordinary oven. These plastics are usually available in the form of sheets, rods and tubes for further working.

The thermosetting types cannot be further formed by the application of heat and pressure. They undergo a chemical change when they are first subjected to heat and pressure and are thereby converted into insoluble, infusible masses. They do not stretch to permit reforming.

Distinguishing Characteristics

Plastics are available in inexhaustible varieties of colors, textures and forms. These range from soft, tacky semi-liquids to flexible fibers and sheets, and rigid solids such as rods, tubes and blocks of any conceivable size and shape. Some plastics are so colorless and crystal-clear that the material is almost invisible; others are translucent or opaque. Some are impeccably smooth; others are rough or patterned in texture. Most plastic materials are resistant to water, acids and alcohol. Although more and more plastics are made to imitate natural materials, their resilience, coldness and aroma usually distinguish them from most natural materials.

Cutting Processes

CUTTING WITH SCISSORS. The thermoplastic material can be cut with ordinary scissors when it is heated to a limp bending point. Follow the specific instructions for heating as given under manipulative possibilities.

CARVING. To avoid cracking, heat the plastic until warm. Hold the piece in a bench stop or clamp the piece securely. Use gouges and other wood-carving tools to chip away small particles at a time. For deeper cuts, use a mallet and chisels.

DRILLING. Use standard hand drills as for wood or metal. In drilling holes, use soap as a lubricant to prevent clogging and sticking of the drill. Also, withdraw the drill from the hole frequently to remove the shavings and to allow the drill to cool. Drill slowly with light pressure. When a high-speed power drill is used, water should be used as a coolant.

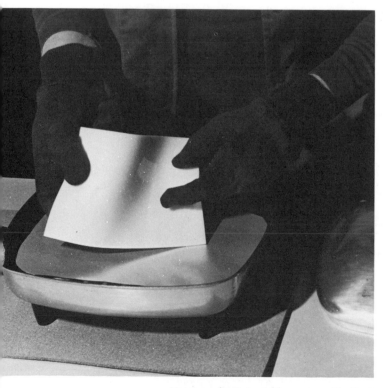

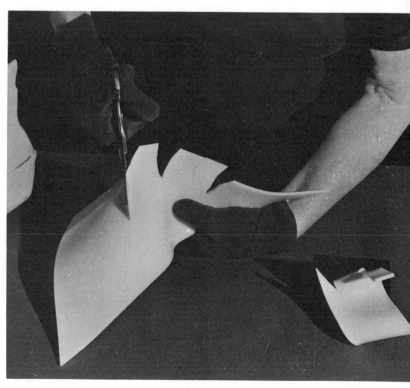

Heating plastic in table oven until pliant.　　Cutting heated plastic with scissors.

Plastic experiments: fastening possibilities. Caging, cementing, doweling, lacing, riveting and screwing.

Fastening Process

CEMENTING. Use the solvent for the particular type of plastic to cement it. This makes for the strongest kind of binding as it is integral to the material itself.

Most thermoplastics, such as lucite and plexiglass, are soluble in ethylene dichloride solvent. Acetate plastics are soluble in acetone solvent. Avoid inhaling the fumes from these solvents. Work in a well-ventilated room. Pieces to be joined must be clean and fit accurately. Use the solvent to dissolve and soften the surfaces to be joined. Then, press the surfaces together until the solvent evaporates. This takes only a few minutes. The pieces should set and harden with a clean, clear joint.

Try various ways to apply the solvent. One possibility is to use the pointed end of a plastic rod as an applicator. The solvent simultaneously dissolves some of the applicator as well as the surfaces to be joined. Another approach is to immerse the edge of one of the two pieces to be joined in the solvent. Use a clean glass or metal dish which is just barely coated with a little of the solvent. Hold the edge in the solvent about five minutes until the surface is softened. Place the softened edge on the other piece of plastic carefully to avoid smearing. Work quickly before the solvent evaporates. Hold the pieces firmly in the same position until the joint is set. Release your hold in a few minutes, but do not handle the piece until it is thoroughly hardened.

Plastic experiments: cutting and manipulative possibilities.

Thick plastic carved after being heated.

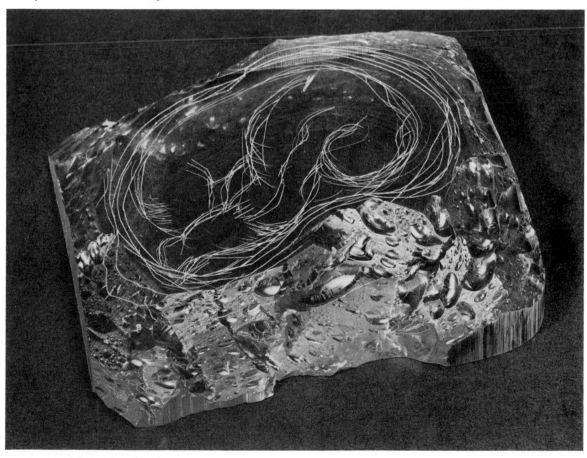

Bending thick plastic after heating.

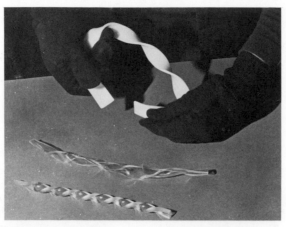
Twisting heated plastic.

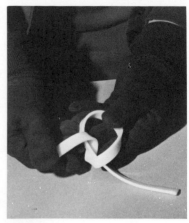
Tying knots in heated plastic.

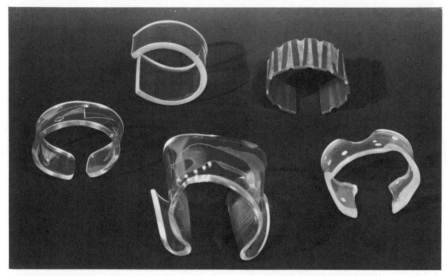
Plastic bracelets. Various methods of surface treatment: drilling, filing and inscribing. These were done before heating the plastic to make the bends and curves.

Manipulative Possibilities

BENDING, TWISTING AND TYING. The thermoplastics, such as lucite and plexiglass, can easily be manipulated and formed after heating at moderate temperatures in an ordinary oven.

Remove the protective paper from the plastic before heating it. Place the plastic on a cookie sheet lined with aluminum foil. Preheat the oven at 350°F. Allow approximately ½ hour to heat through small thin pieces (⅛″ to ¼″ thick). Increase the time proportionately for thicker and larger pieces. The timing is not too critical, but avoid overheating to the point that the material sticks to the foil or pan. It is best to experiment with small pieces to get acquainted with the timing and process. The material should be heated until it is limp. Use protective heat-proof kitchen mitts to handle it.

The plastic retains the heat for several minutes. Experiment with rolling, twisting and bending it. If a result is not satisfactory, return the plastic to the oven and it will unbend to its original flat shape. Thermoplastics have a "plastic memory." Any piece which has been manipulated will revert to its original shape. It is especially exciting to see strips that have been tied up in knots become untied when they are put back in the oven!

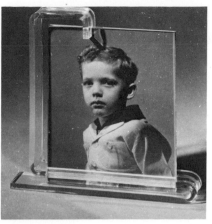

Plastic picture frame. The structure allows for quick removal and changes of pictures.

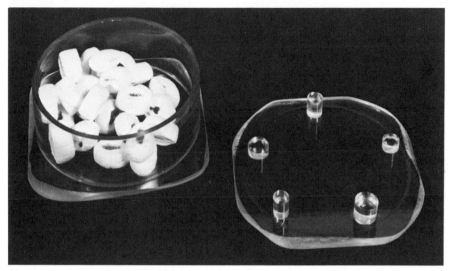

Plastic container with cover. An example of spatial projection of surfaces attached with plastic cement.

FORMING. To achieve a definite, preplanned shape or to make several identical pieces, it is necessary to use a form. Forms can be made of wood, cardboard or plaster, but they should be sanded smooth or covered with smooth cloth or paper. Otherwise, the heated plastic will take the impression of any scratches or seams. Cut the plastic slightly larger than the finished shape is to be, to allow for shrinkage that results from bending. When the plastic is heated to a limp state, press it over the form and leave it to cool.

CASTING. Commercially prepared liquid casting plastics are especially manufactured for use in molds. They can also be used to embed photographs, stones and other "found" objects and specimens.

DISSOLVING. Thermoplastics can be dissolved to a liquid state. Use ethylene dichloride solvent to dissolve plexiglass or lucite. Use acetone solvent to dissolve acetate plastics. Cut the plastic into small pieces or use shavings or scraps. Pour enough of the liquid solvent to cover the scraps. Use a bottle or jar with a cover. It is important to keep it covered, as the solvent evaporates immediately. To make a thin liquid plastic, use more solvent. Small pieces usually dissolve in 10 to 15 minutes. The dissolved plastic can be used as a cement or for casting in molds.

Surface Treatment

PAINTING. Use enamels, lacquers, or plastic-base paints. Other paints will chip or peel off.

DYEING. Use plastic dyes. These are made of a combination of solvent and dye and penetrate the plastic material. Keep the plastic immersed until the desired intensity is reached. Laminating dyes serve a dual purpose. They are a means of fastening and coloring simultaneously. Follow the same instructions for cementing, but use laminating dyes instead of the clear solvent.

TAKING IMPRESSIONS. When plastic is heated to a limp state, it can be impressed with shapes and textures of screen wire, nail heads, screw heads or any patterned tools.

LIGHT AND COLOR PIPING. Clear plastics, such as lucite and plexiglass, have unusual optical properties. The material conducts light and color invisibly through polished surfaces and "delivers" it to any sanded surfaces on the opposite edges of the piece. (See Color Plate 30.) This property makes the material particularly suitable for decorative lighting and luminous signs.

Finishing

CLEANING. Naphtha or dry-cleaning fluid can be used to remove grease or oil spots or to remove smudges left by protective masking paper. Follow with a soap and water washing.

Soap and towel holder. Experimental design. The experiment and the material are especially suitable for the purpose.

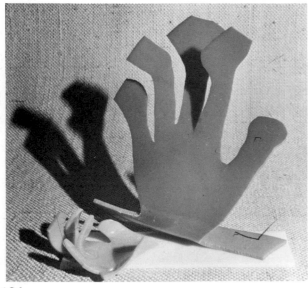

SANDPAPERING. Use sandpaper or garnet paper to remove deep scratches. Wrap the paper around a wooden block or piece of cork for surface sanding. Use water with waterproof sandpaper to reduce the heat of friction. Sand with a rotating motion to avoid streaks. Avoid excess pressure. Do not sand unless absolutely necessary. Minor scratches "disappear" with ashing and waxing.

ASHING. Use an abrasive like powdered pumice, or much finer abrasives, such as whiting or toothpaste. Apply the abrasive with a cloth or chamois, using a circular motion.

POLISHING AND BUFFING. Use "anti-static" liquid wax made especially for plastics, or the cleaners and waxes made for automobile polishing. Buff the surface with a soft flannel cloth until it is crystal clear.

(Left below) Plexiglass lamp with aluminum tube base. The design was carefully planned to utilize the unique properties of plastic for light transmission.

(Center below) Plastic sand timer. A structure for color transmission. The parts were simultaneously fastened and colored with laminating dyes and then carved both internally and externally. The clear plastic conducts color to any cut surfaces and causes changeable color combinations from different viewpoints and different lighting. Four-dimensional changes in image are achieved by reversing the position of the timer and the movement of the sand within it. (Reverse position is shown in Color Plate 31.)

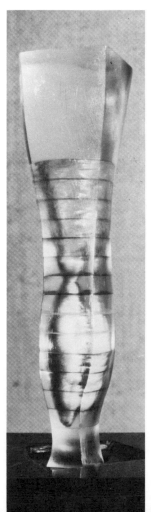

Plexiglass lamp-table. This dual-purpose design was preplanned in every detail. The pieces and parts are precisely fitted together for structural strength. The decorative tissue paper collage screens the bulb to emphasize the transmission of light through the plastic edges. (See Color Plate 33.)

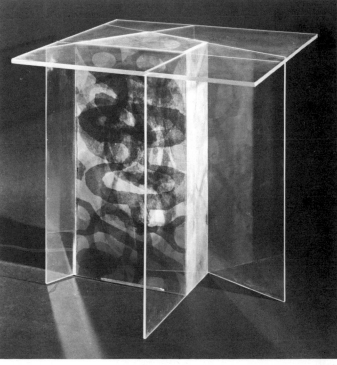

Wood of many types and forms.

A plentiful supply of wood motivates interest and ideas.

WOOD

Source and Method of Production

The hard inner substance that makes up the greater part of tree trunks is the source of wood. Cellulose is the basic substance; lignin is the stiffening or bonding agent. The patterns of grain are partly due to the way that the wood is cut from logs and made into lumber. When sawed tangent to the growth rings, it is flat-grained; when sawed radially or "quarter-sawed," it is edge-grained. To prevent warping and twisting, wood is seasoned until its moisture content is compatible to the humidity of the location where it is to be used. Natural air drying, kiln drying and chemical drying are used depending on the time available and ultimate use of the wood.

Distinguishing Characteristics

Wood is not a homogenous substance; its structure is highly variable, depending upon the species, climate, growth rate and moisture content. The grain, figure, texture and color are especially interesting because of their variability. Structural formations and even defects affect and enhance the appearance of wood. Spiral growth results in a winding stripe; butt wood shows the assembly of root branches; crotch figures come from the Y-shaped forks formed at the joinings of branches to trunks; burl figures and shapes are a result of the large wart-like growths on the trunk.

The terms "hardwood" and "softwood" have no direct application to the hardness or softness of the wood. These terms pertain to the classification of native species of trees. Native softwoods come from coniferous evergreens, while native hardwoods come from deciduous, leaf-shedding trees.

Veneers, which are the thinnest splits of wood, similar to the weight of paper, are especially adaptive for inlaying. When veneers are fabricated with a paper or cloth backing, they are less inclined to split and are much easier to cut into intricate shapes. Veneer edging, which is paper-backed and available in ribbon-like rolls, is one of the most efficient and inexpensive sources for a diversity of wood grains, patterns and colors.

Types of Wood Suitable for Crafts

Domestic woods such as redwood, pine, fir, cedar, balsam, basswood, cypress, walnut, cherry, apple and other fruitwoods are very versatile for many craft purposes. Imported woods such as mahogany, ebony, rosewood, and teakwood are more suitable for small craft objects and jewelry.

Most of these woods can be procured in a variety of thicknesses and forms. Solid blocks from one to four inches thick are best for one-piece carving and for lathe-turning squares. Thin sheets of solid stock, which are only ⅛″ and ¼″ thick, should be reserved for small objects, as they are inclined to warp and split in larger sizes. When large pieces of thin wood are needed, it is best to use plywood, a built-up wood product of three or more layers. Warping is counteracted by alternating the direction of the grain for each successive layer. Also, plywood can be faced with veneers of rare and more interesting grains and textures.

The examples of experiments and finished craft objects show how the basic tools and processes for cutting, fastening, manipulation and surface treatment have been utilized for structuring a wide variety of types of wood.

Wood experiments: various cutting possibilities.

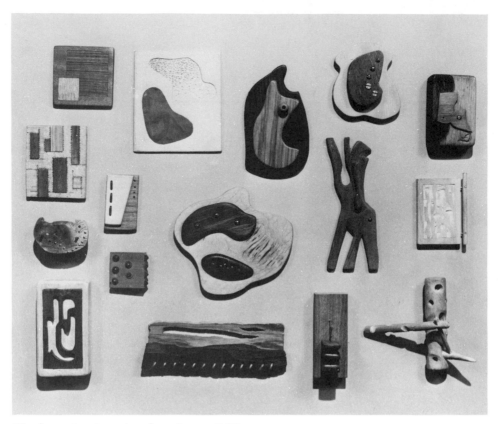

Wood experiments: various fastening possibilities.

Rosy-red Rump Roost by Valenza, 1969. Wood stained crimson red; 15" high. An example of three-dimensional carving of a one-piece form featuring the natural formations and grain patterns of wood. (Photo: U.N.H.)

(Far left) Persian ceremonial spoons. An example of restraint and delicacy in cutting and carving. One-piece subtractive edge cutting and internal cutting and carving with surface incising. Subjective floral and geometric motifs. (Collection: Roy Jinstrom.)

(Left) Nut server. Yugoslavian Folk Art. One-piece subtractive carving and incised surface cutting. Subjective bird motif.

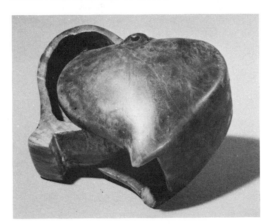

(Far left) Rattle of movable seeds. Peking, China, 1920–30. A participatory structure of birchwood. (Courtesy: The Field Museum of Natural History, Chicago.)

(Left) Toggle box. Peking, China, 1920–30. A kinetic structure carved from a peachwood burl. (Courtesy: The Field Museum of Natural History, Chicago.)

Ceremonial wood spoon. Luzon, Philippines; Ifugao Tribe. One-piece subtractive structure achieved by edge cutting, internal cutting and surface cutting. Subjective motif. (Courtesy: The Field Museum of Natural History, Chicago.)

Oil dish. Cameroon, Africa. An example of a one-piece subtractive structure achieved by edge cutting, internal cutting and carving and decorative surface cutting. (Courtesy: The Museum of Primitive Art, New York.)

(Above) A group of wood experiments converted to candle-holders by Charles Kaplan.

(Left) Sculptural egg holders. Experimental design. This practical use for the wood experiments highlights the sculptural forms.

(Below) Stamp and letter holder. Experimental design. The shapes and forms of the things that are held relate to the size and scale of the experimental structure.

Laminated wood structure by Charles Kaplan. Overlays of wood joined with white emulsion glue. Edge cutting and carving on a lathe reveals contrasting grains and colors of the laminated wood.

Wood experiment: additive structures. Various fastening processes were used to attach the carved forms: cementing, doweling and wedging. Surface treatment includes burning, coloring and coating with wax.

Chess set. Preplanned design. The designs for the chessmen and the board were directly inspired by the processes and techniques used in the experiment on the previous page. The reverse side of the board (shown above) is a sculptural structure of three-dimensional overlays of low relief.

Wood tray. Yellow pine. The ordinary piece of wood encouraged direct cutting and burning of the surface.

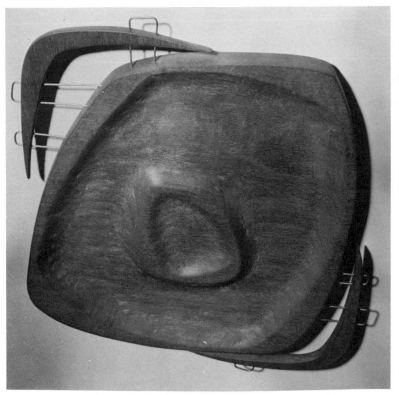

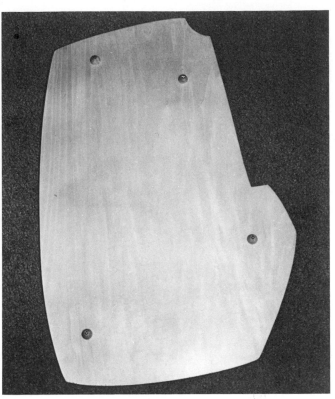

Wood tray. Mahogany and brass. After spontaneous cutting and carving of the shapes and forms, the leftover pieces of wood were adapted into handles with fastenings of brass wire through drilled holes.

Reverse side of the tray reproduced in color (Plate 27). The reverse side shows the sensitive shaping of the contour that can be achieved with a hand saw.

Wood tray. Veneered plywood with interlacing of reed over spokes of dowel rods.

Raffia and reed of various textures and widths.

Raffia experiments: coil binding.

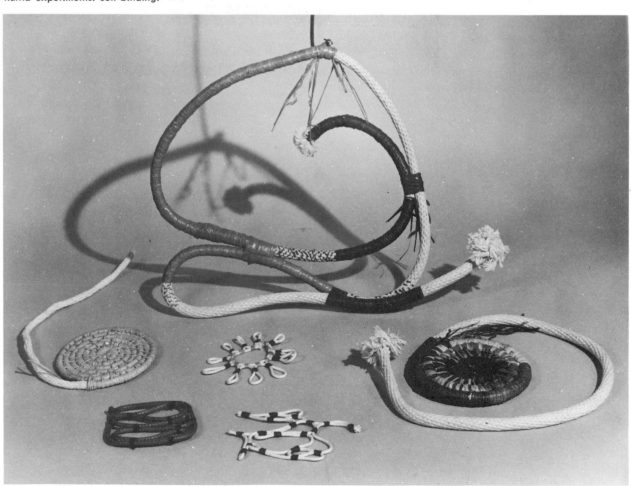

CHAPTER 9/Crafts of Linear Materials: Raffia and Reed, Cord and Rope, Wire

Linear materials are continuous strands, strips or bands of material moving in two directions. They are available in varying degrees of flexibility and firmness, depending on the source and type of material from which they are derived. Some are of round shapes of various diameters; others are flat strips of various widths.

Raffia and reed are natural plant peelings and cuttings. Cords and ropes are made of twisted or braided fibers from both natural and synthetic sources. Wire is the linear form of metal. It is extruded from all types of metals and alloys and takes on their respective characteristics of hardness and malleability.

Flexible materials of linear form are especially suitable for manipulation into continuous line structures. These can be used to create flat two-dimensional shapes as well as for three- and four-dimensional forms.

Most of the techniques and processes can be done entirely by hand. Only a few ordinary household tools like scissors, shears and pliers are needed to start and finish the work. Specific instructions for cutting and fastening methods are given with the various manipulative processes for each type of material.

RAFFIA AND REED

These linear materials of fibrous structure are considered together because of their compatibility for numerous utilitarian purposes. Each contributes to the other in structuring shapes and forms that withstand weathering and wear under similar conditions.

Source and Method of Production

Raffia is the stringy fibrous peeling of the raffia palm tree which thrives in the area of Madagascar. The peelings are tied into bundles of fairly uniform lengths of about three to four feet. Modern methods of processing usually include dyeing and waxing. The colors are generally subtle. Synthetic materials are now being used to produce strands of material that simulate the texture of raffia. These offer some advantages over the natural material in that they are available in a much wider range of colors and in longer lengths of continuous strands.

Reed is a cutting of any of various tall, bamboo-like grasses that abound in tropical climates. The outer coating is cut into ribbon-like strips. The inner core is processed in various diameters.

Distinguishing Characteristics

Raffia is a flexible, irregular material characterized by a shaggy splitting of the fiber into variable widths and textures. This natural variability gives it a casual quality. It is inclined to split and splinter when dry and needs to be moistened to make it pliant. However, raffia that is waxed in processing is flexible and easy to work without moistening.

Reed is generally smooth on the outer surface. It is brittle and breakable when dry and must be soaked in water until it is pliable for manipulation.

Since the linear and flexible characteristics predominate, the manipulative processes are most suitable for work with raffia and reed. Most of the processes can be done by hand alone. Only a few ordinary tools and binding materials are needed: scissors, needles, thread and masking tape. The work is portable and can be done at a leisurely pace; it can be left at any point and picked up again at will.

Coil binding. Straw and palm leaf. Egyptian, 18th Dynasty. (Courtesy: The Metropolitan Museum of Art.)

Sandals. Coil binding of papyrus, palm leaf and grass. Egyptian, Thebes, 18th Dynasty. (Courtesy: The Metropolitan Museum of Art.)

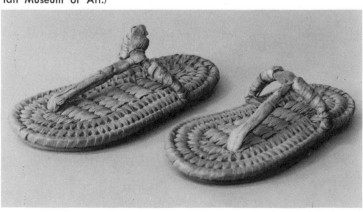

Raffia body jewelry. Discs of coil binding. Contemporary use of an ancient material and process. (Courtesy: Conde Nast Publications; Vogue.)

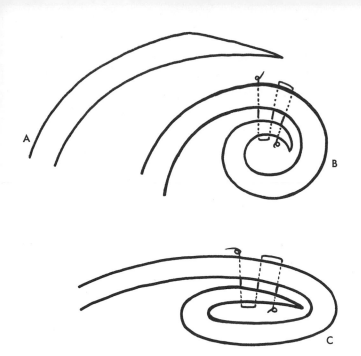

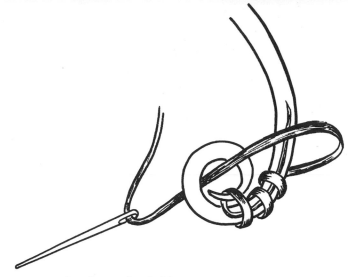

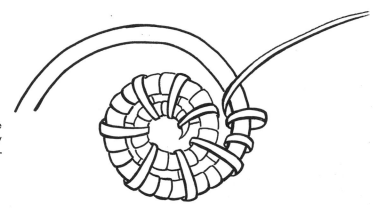

Making the Coil Button
(A) Cut rope at tapered angle.
(B) and (C) Round and oval shaped buttons. Sew the end of the rope in position with a few stitches of heavy button or carpet thread. These stitches can be concealed later by the binding process.

Lazy Squaw Stitch
Wind around the coil two or three times and then stitch into the row below. Place the stitches radially toward the center of the coil button.

Developing the Coil Button
Enlarge the button by spiral winding of rope and alternate binding with raffia. Conceal the end of raffia under the binding.

Manipulative Processes: Raffia

COIL BINDING WITH RAFFIA. Use rope of about ¼″ diameter. Ordinary clothesline is excellent for this process. Use a blunt-point or tapestry needle for the raffia.

MAKING THE COIL BUTTON. The coil button is usually round, but can also be oval, square, triangular or irregular. To facilitate the shaping of the button, cut the rope at a tapered angle for about an inch. Sew it in position with a few stitches of heavy button or carpet thread. These stitches are later concealed by the raffia binding. (See the diagram.)

DEVELOPING THE BUTTON. Gradually enlarge the button by spirally winding the coil of rope around itself and alternately binding it with stitches of raffia. Keep the stitches and the distance between them uniform to create a rhythmic pattern. Place the stitches radially toward the center of the button. (See the diagrams for three basic types of stitches: lazy-squaw stitch, single-knot stitch and double-knot stitch.)

LAZY-SQUAW STITCH. After making the coil button, continue to wind the raffia around the coil two or three times and then stitch into the raffia in the row below. The number of times to wrap is determined by the width of the strand of raffia. The width and weight of natural raffia is unpredictable. However, the synthetic strands are of uniform width.

SINGLE-KNOT STITCH. After making the coil button, follow the same initial instructions as for lazy squaws, but bring the needle to the top, in between the unwrapped part of the coil and the wrapped part of the row below. Then, stitch back across the last long stitch. This makes a knot on the top surface only.

DOUBLE-KNOT STITCH. Follow the instructions for the single-knot stitch, but before stitching across the last long stitch, wrap the un-wrapped coil once more. This brings the needle back between the wrapped and unwrapped coil. Then, stitch back across the last long stitch from top down and around so that the knot shows on both the top and the bottom sides.

CREATING THE CONTOUR. Place successive rows of coil binding over each other to build up the work to the height and form desired. For subtle gradation in the shaping of the side walls, project the new coil of rope halfway over the previous row. Because of the flexibility of the rope and raffia, it is easy to change directions inward and outward. (See the sketches for various possibilities.)

CHANGING COLOR. Hold the work in the left hand with a supply of rope to the left. Hold the short end of a new strand parallel to the rope. Use the long end of the new strand to bind over the short end, and the rope to secure the new strand in position. Continue to carry the previous color parallel to the rope and wrap over it, to conceal it along with the rope, for use as desired. Since the strands are carried along continuously, the changes in color can be made easily and securely without any cutting or knotting.

MAKING HANDLES AND LOOPS. The handles can be made separately and attached by stitching with raffia over the form. Another way is to continue the coil binding to the point of the handle and then separate the binding from the form for several inches as desired, before rejoining the stitching to the last row of coil binding.

ENDING AND FINISHING. Cut the rope at a taper for one inch. Continue to bind and stitch with raffia far enough over the last coil to make it secure. Tie the raffia into a secure knot and bring back the ends through the coil in between the raffia and rope.

Pot stand. Egyptian, 18th Dynasty. An example of contour shaping. (Courtesy: The Metropolitan Museum of Art.)

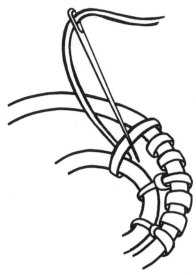

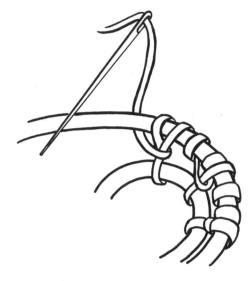

Single-Knot Stitch
Wind around the coil two or three times and stitch into the row below. Then, bring the needle to the top and stitch back across the last long stitch. This makes a knot on the top surface.

Double-Knot Stitch
Wind around the coil two or three times and stitch into the row below. Then, wrap around the coil once more. This brings the needle in position to cross over and around the last long stitch and makes a knot on both sides of the coil binding.

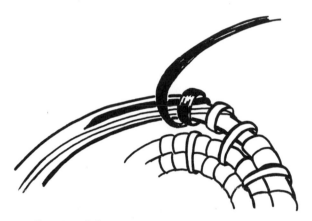

Changing Color
Hold work in left hand with supply of rope to left. Hold short end of the new strand of color parallel to the rope. Use the long end of the new color to bind over the short end and the rope to secure the new strand in position. Also, continue to carry the previous color parallel to the rope and wrap over it to conceal it. Two or more strands of color can be carried along the rope continuously and changes of color can be made easily and securely.

Making Handles and Loops
Continue the coil binding to the point of the handle. Separate the binding from the form for several inches as desired before rejoining the stitching to the last row of coil binding.

Contour Shaping
Overlay successive rows of coil binding to build up work to the desired height and form. To change the shape either inward or outward, project the new row halfway over the previous row.

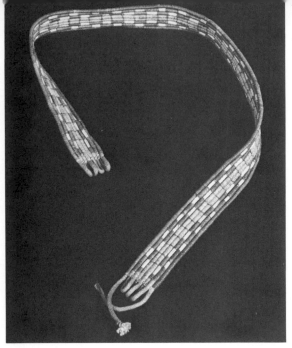

Raffia belt. Coil binding using the double-knot stitch.

Raffia sandals. Coil binding using the lazy squaw stitch.

Basket. New Mexico. Coil binding with reed core; 13" high. An example of shaping of contour by gradual changes in the placement of successive rows of the coil. (Courtesy: The Museum of Primitive Art, New York.)

Sculptural stand for hats, wigs or jewelry. Raffia wrapping over a foundation of cardboard and foam plastic.

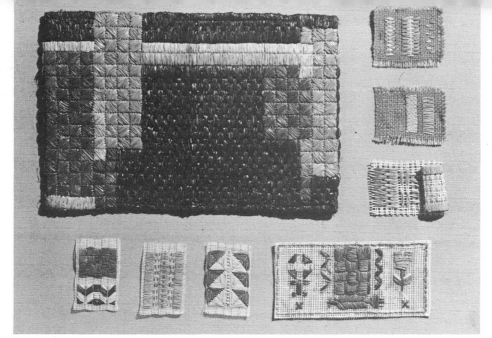

Raffia stitchery on canvas and burlap.

RAFFIA STITCHERY. Use needlepoint canvas or various loosely woven mesh types of fabric or burlap as a base material. Use a blunt-point or tapestry needle to thread the strands of raffia. Avoid stitches more than ½″ in length, to prevent catching or pulling. Try geometric designs based on squares or rectangles that relate to the woven mesh of the fabrics.

RAFFIA WRAPPING. Wrap strands of raffia around segments of cardboard tubing or cigar boxes or disks with a center hole. This is a quick method of concealing the cardboard without using any adhesives. Tie knots to change colors. The knots can easily be concealed under the wrapping or they can be utilized as part of the pattern.

Manipulative Processes: Reed

After the reed is soaked, it can be manipulated freely to create structures of irregular shapes and forms. These can be fastened with wire, cord or other strands of reed or raffia.

INTERLACING. Three or more firm strands of reed can be used as spokes for interlacing. Flexible strands of raffia or fibers or reed can be used as weft to pass over and under the successive spokes.

For square and rectangular shapes, arrange the spokes evenly from left to right. For circular shapes, use an uneven number of spokes and arrange them radially from the center.

Interlacing can be used to create flat two-dimensional mats or for three-dimensional containers.

COMBINING WITH RIGID MATERIALS. For a quick method of making containers and similar structures, use a base of rigid material such as wood, cork or compressed wallboard. Drill holes along the edge of the base. Then, insert spokes of reed in the holes. These spokes can be attached with glue or twisted around the adjacent spoke. Then, alternately weave the weft strands of reed or raffia over and under the spokes. This method may be seen in the illustration of the tray on page 143.

Bamboo basket. Contemporary Japanese. Three-dimensional structure formed by bending dampened bamboo reed and binding with finer reed.

Bamboo steaming basket. Hong Kong. A four-dimensional structure seen in two views: assembled and the parts separated. The assembled form features structural motifs for decoration. The separate forms can be combined to create changes in image.

Egg basket. Oaxaca, Mexico. An example of a practical, utilitarian object with sculptural quality. The open view shows the interlaced structure made of different widths and diameters of reed. (Collection: Mr. and Mrs. George Tagge.)

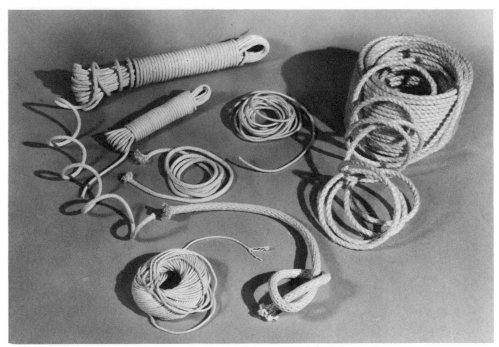

Common types of cord and rope. Various weights and textures and different kinds of fibers twisted or braided together.

CORD AND ROPE

Source and Method of Production

Cords and ropes are made of fibers twisted or braided together for strength and durability. They are produced in various diameters, weights, textures and colors. The rigidity and flexibility depend on the methods of braiding and twisting that are used in their formation.

Distinguishing Characteristics

The colors and textures of the different kinds of cords and ropes reveal the characteristics and qualities of the fibrous materials that were used in their production. They are coarse, irregular and springy when made of sisal, manila and jute. They are much more pliant and soft when made of cotton and flax. And they can be much more lustrous and uniform when made of synthetic fibers.

Manipulation and Fastening Methods

BINDING AND TYING. Place a length of the material on a piece of cardboard or drawing board. Manipulate it freely to get acquainted with its flexibility and spring. Try spiral, figure-eight and space-filling shapes. Try circles, ovals, triangles and irregular shapes. Hold the shapes in position temporarily with masking tape. At this stage, it is possible to make adjustments in details. For a permanent hold, use raffia or heavy thread to bind the rope together at intervals. Tie the binding material securely with a double knot. The ends of the binding can be concealed under the binding or allowed to show as a decorative feature. This method is especially effective when the rope is bound only at points where binding is needed to hold the shape of the design. The rope is the dominant material.

153

Rope of twisted crepe paper wrapped over a coffee can. Library paste was used for fastening as the winding progressed. Several coats of shellac were applied for a protective finish and for more permanent adhesion.

SEWING. Use rope as a foundation, as above, but join it at intervals by sewing through the rope with a strong button or carpet thread. In this method, the stitching can be kept invisible as the thread can be concealed within the rope. To feature the stitches as a decorative element, use a contrasting color of thread. Also add knots, beads and other contrasting materials.

WRAPPING OVER FORMS. Use any ready-made or salvaged forms such as glass bottles, plastic detergent bottles, cardboard cartons or metal cans. To attach one end of rope securely, unravel the end for about an inch. Then, spread it out and stick it down with plastic china cement. Wrap over this end and continue to wrap until the entire form is covered. Finish by cementing the end or tying it into position with a decorative knot or fringe.

Color or texture changes can be introduced by cementing other strands of rope at intervals, but the one long continuous strand of rope should be carried along with the new colors to assure strength and durability. It is also possible to sew through the rope to hold it in position without any cementing.

Kinetic puzzle. Rope binding over a wire foundation.

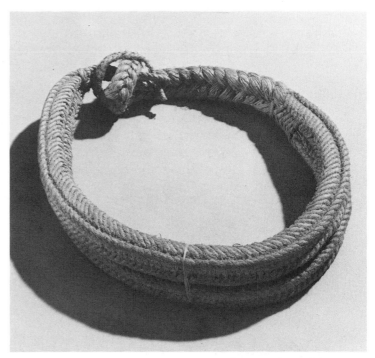

Rope belt. A braided structure. Congo (Kinshasa), Southern Kasai Province. (Courtesy: The Museum of Primitive Art. Gift of Homer Pyle.)

Manipulation and fastening of rope: binding and tying.

Coasters from the market in Nassau, Bahamas. Manipulation and fastening of sisal cord with sewing.

MACRAMÉ KNOTTING. Use a fairly heavy, but limp, rope to get acquainted with the knotting processes. Avoid ropes that have too much spring and bristle. To support the work, use a drapery or dowel rod or a piece of heavier rope such as clothesline for a "holding line." Attach this to a piece of porous wallboard in a horizontal position.

Hang two or more tying cords over this holding line at the center so that the ends hang even. Try a few simple basic knots such as the spiral knot, half-knot, and square knot. (See diagrams.) Repeat any one of these knots until you can see the evolution of a rhythmic pattern. These three basic knots can be combined and varied in numerous creative ways.

To finish the piece, work the loose ends back into the last row of knots with a blunt needle or any pointed tool. Use some plastic cement to hold the ends in position. When the cement is dry, trim off the excess cord. Replace the holding line at the start of the piece with a buckle or ring or a piece of wire, depending on the ultimate use of the piece.

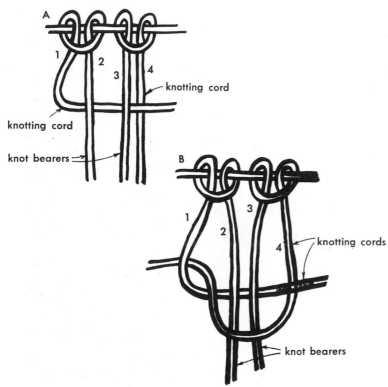

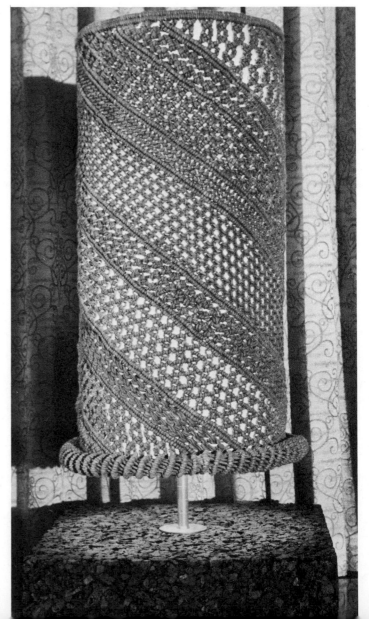

Macramé lamp with cork base by Joan Paque. The wire frame of the shade was used as the holding line for tying and knotting the cord in diagonal border patterns.

Spiral Knot, Half Knot, Square Knot

(A) Make "L" with the left-hand cord (1) going under cords 2 and 3 and over 4.

(B) Take the right-hand cord (4) and put it through the loop formed on the left and pull both taut. This two-step sequence is varied to create the spiral, half and square knot patterns as follows:

Spiral Knot. The sequence is started and continuously done from either the left side (as illustrated), or the right side. (Thus, the "L" is started left, left, left, left, etc. Or, right, right, right, etc.)

Half Knot. The "L" is formed first on one side and then on the other. (Left, right, left, right, left, right, etc.) Having formed the "L" from the left-hand side (as illustrated), then start the sequence from the right. Cord 1 forms the "L" going under 3, under 2, and over 4. Cord 4 crosses over 2 and 3 and goes through the loop formed by 1.

Square Knot. Results when the "L" sequence is begun first on one side, then on the other, and finally on the first side again. (Left, right, left. Left, right, left. Left, right, left, and so on.)

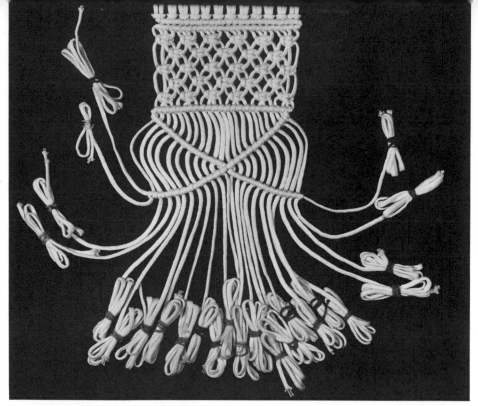

Macramé knotting in progress by Jacquelin Dodson.

Macramé necklace by Lisa Kores.

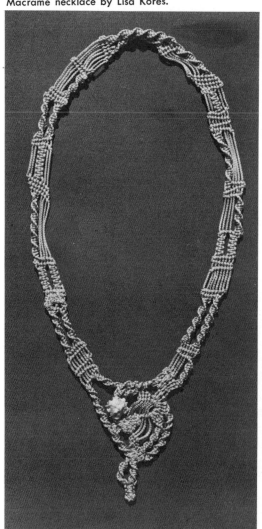

Macramé by Joan Paque. Diversity of patterns are derived from a few basic knots.

Macramé necklace by Leslie Myers. (Courtesy: West Genesee Senior High School, Camillus, New York.)

WIRE

Source and Method of Production

Wire is a linear form of metal. It is produced in various gauges or diameters and in various degrees of flexibility. It is usually circular in cross section. It ranges in gauge from slender thread-like types to heavy rod-like forms. Aluminum, copper, brass, bronze, iron, nickel, silver and steel are commonly available in wire form. The flexibility of wire depends on the hardness or softness of the metal and its alloy content.

Wire is produced in a wide variety of types. Stranded wire consists of two or more fine strands of wire twisted together for added strength and flexibility. Picture-cord wire is a typical example. Wire is often coated with other materials such as rubber, plastic and fibers. Stem wire, which is coated with fluffy chenille fibers, is available in brilliant colors and is suitable for many craft projects. Wire screening or wire cloth, which is made by interlacing strands of wire, also offers many possibilities for craftmaking.

Distinguishing Characteristics

The flexibility of wire is its most distinguishing feature. Unlike most other linear materials, such as cords and ropes, it can be bent and twisted into a firm, secure position without tying.

Fastening Methods for Wire

TWISTING. Twisting is the quickest and most expedient method of fastening wire. It makes a firm and secure joint and also allows for adjustments and unfastening.

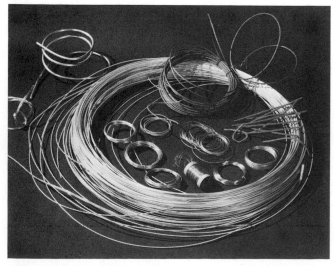
Wire of various metals and gauges.

Ear ornaments of silver wire. Indonesia. (Courtesy: The Museum of Primitive Art, New York.)

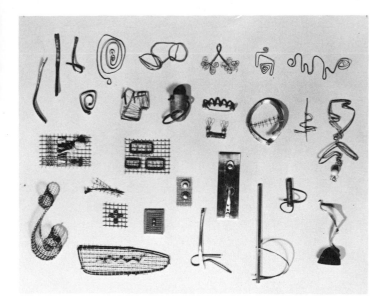

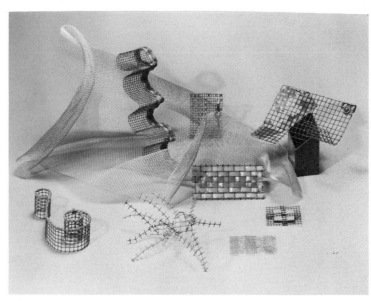

Wire experiments: cutting, manipulation and fastening.   Screen wire experiments: cutting, manipulation and fastening.

INTERLACING. Fine gauges of wire can be interlaced through holes that have been drilled in heavier wire, rods and other materials. The ends can be flattened by hammering to serve as a locking device.

SOLDERING. Soldering is the most secure method of fastening wire. Follow instructions for soldering metal (page 112).

FASTENING TO OTHER MATERIALS. First flatten the wire with a hammer at the point where it is to be attached. Then, drill a hole through the wire to insert the fastener. Nails, screws, rivets and other metal fasteners can be used to attach wire to metal and other rigid materials.

Manipulation

Flexible wire can be manipulated freehand. Use pliers to bend stiff wire. Round-nose pliers and long-chain pliers are essential for the small bends usually needed in jewelry making.

Wire screening of fine mesh can be modeled and shaped into sculptural forms. Use a small, rounded wood rod or the eraser on the end of an ordinary pencil to push against the mesh and force it into relief formations.

Surface Treatment

PAINTING. Enamels, lacquers or acrylic paints can be used to create design patterns on wire screening. Use graph paper to plan designs with a squared motif. Apply paint thick enough to fill in some of the holes of the screening to contrast with areas of clear mesh.

TEXTURING. The larger widths and diameters of wire, such as those under number 12 gauge, are suitable for decorative texturing. Use files to make scratches or grooves at intervals. Use a ball peen hammer for a blended, hammered effect.

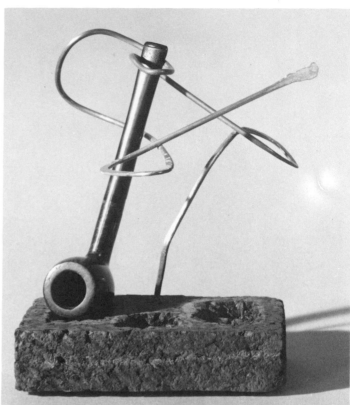

Wire experiment and conversion of the experiment into a pipe holder. After manipulation and hammering, the wire was inserted into a hole in the cork base. As a holder for three pipes several changes of the visible form are possible.

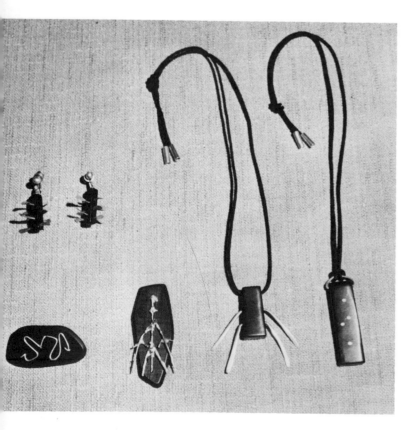

(Above) *Shaggy Dog.* Edge cutting and manipulation of one piece of flexible screen wire that was then interlaced with raffia.

(Left) Solderless jewelry. Manipulation and embedding of wire in ebony.

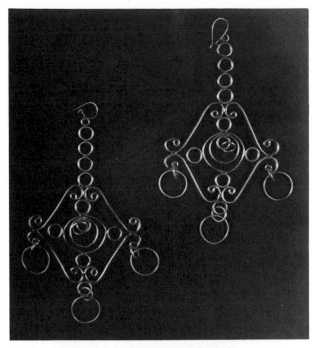

Earrings of silver wire by Harun Abdulrashid.

Buckle by Alexander Calder, before 1943. Hammered brass. A mobile structure of limited movement for a functional purpose. (Collection: The Museum of Modern Art, New York. Gift of the artist.)

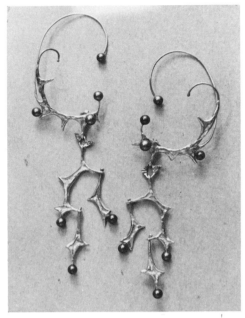

Wire earrings with pearls by Freda Koerper.

Necklace of silver wire with ebony terminals. Spontaneous design. The ebony was drilled and shaped with a feel for the grain of the wood. The hammered ends of the wire serve as a decorative locking device.

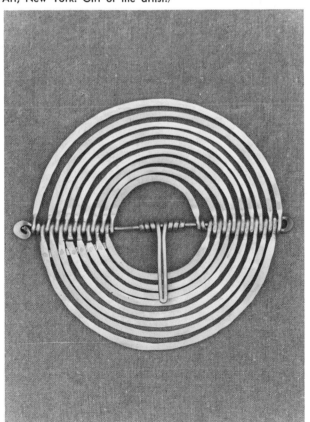

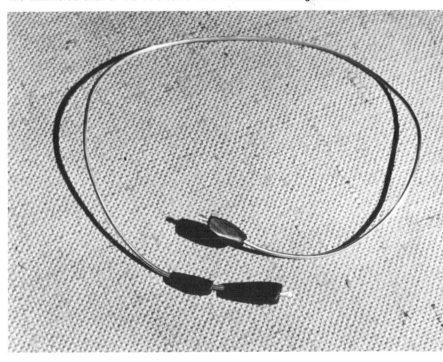

PART FOUR
AN EVALUATIVE VIEW

Comb by Alexander Calder, before 1943. (Collection: The Museum of Modern Art, New York. Gift of the artist.)

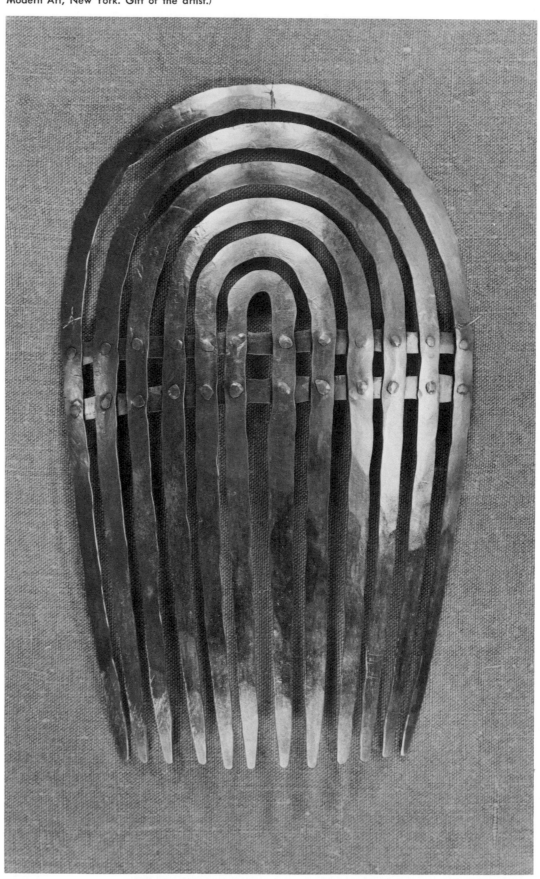

CHAPTER 10 / Toward Appreciation of Crafts

Choosing and Judging Crafts

Most people feel confident about evaluating the quality of a craft object. They "know what they like" and choose and judge accordingly. Their reasons for choice are usually traceable to a reverence for skillful craftsmanship and sentimental associations.

They tend to value the crafts that are neatly and meticulously made as superior to those that are casual or rugged in structure. They are likely to consider things that are complex and were hard to do as far better than those that are simple and were made quickly and easily. They generally rate things made of rare or precious materials as better than those made of common or inexpensive materials. Often, their predilection for "collecting" owls or pussycats and daggers or paperweights outweighs all other factors of judgment.

The New Image of Crafts

The new look of crafts has upset the usual standards of judgment. It dispels the common criteria as not necessarily true. It honors wide-ranging differences in style and technique of workmanship as well as in attitudes about materials and content. With its emphasis on the personally expressive qualities of the useful object, it has aroused a new awareness of the kinship between the crafts and art. It has upgraded the image of crafts from a decorative "minor art" to a significant art form.

The increasing recognition of crafts as art has done much to erase the old-time barriers between the arts. Museums are taking the craft objects out of remote, hard-to-find galleries and allocating more time, space and attention to exhibit them. It is no longer surprising to have a crafts show scheduled as the feature show of the year.

Enduring Criteria

To develop an appreciation for craft objects that deserve this kind of recognition, it is important to evaluate them in terms of the same criteria that are fundamental in the appraisal of the visual arts in general:

(1) Respect for material.

(2) Suitability for purpose.

(3) Creative originality.

(4) Aesthetic design.

Each of these criteria is involved in both the expression and appreciation of individuality. Just as the craftsman deals with them in the process of making crafts, so the viewer can rely on them as a guide to choosing and judging crafts. They relate to the practical factors of utility as well as to the more subtle and elusive aspects of personal sensitivity and style that are vital to the quality of crafts as art.

These criteria allow the viewer a wide range of options in making choices and decisions. They give him a chance to respond in a personal way that reflects his feelings and preferences as well as his critical judgment. A definition of the scope and meaning of each of the criteria reveals the extent of variability that each one encompasses.

RESPECT FOR MATERIAL

This can best be judged by the extent to which the form and structure of the object reveal the inherent qualities and characteristics of the material. The primary concern is with honesty and sincerity in contrast to imitative deception or concealment.

Craftsmen show their respect for material in many different ways. One may leave a piece of wood in its rough-hewn, rugged state, and another may choose to bring out the subtle quality of the grain and pattern by careful and thorough sanding and finishing. In spite of the wide-ranging differences in treatment, both can be equally respectful of the material.

SUITABILITY FOR PURPOSE

The suitability of a craft object for its purpose is largely determined by its practical usability. However, its functional quality is not necessarily dependent on long-lasting durability. A box, a necklace, or a toy might be made of such durable materials and sturdy construction that it lasts for centuries, and yet, these same items can be designed as expendable throwaways for only brief or even momentary use in celebrations, pageants and festivals. Some of these are self-destructive and planned for only fleeting visibility, as in a spectacular display of fireworks, for example. The quality of the design depends on how effectively the craft object functions for its intended role.

CREATIVE ORIGINALITY

Creative originality derives from imaginative and inventive thinking. It is characterized by willingness to abandon orthodox methods in favor of new and untried possibilities. In evaluating a craft object for its creative originality, it is helpful to consider the extent of deviation from the usual types of structure that have been tried and proved over and over again. It should be noted that the creative quality of the form and structure are not contingent upon how recently the work was done. The oldest of historic examples may excel the latest contemporary work.

AESTHETIC DESIGN

Aesthetic design is concerned with the visual organization of all the component parts of an object. While the emphasis is on the look of the object in contrast to its utility, the quality of the design depends on a unified relationship between them.

The elements of design—line, shape, form, color and texture—serve as the graphic vocabulary for the craftsman. His system of organizing them conveys his ideas and intentions. These may range from extremes of subtle harmony to intensive discord. It is largely because of this broad range of possibilities for aesthetic design that the useful object can become a personally expressive work of art.

The criteria described here are based on the timeless and enduring factors that transcend barriers of time and place. They are relevant to the crafts of primitive peoples as well as those of highly sophisticated cultures. The baskets, bowls, boxes and spoons, the belts, sandals, jewelry and masks that have been made by man throughout the ages are important evidence of his mode of life and his cherished values. They exemplify his persistent need for them and his concern and desire for self-identification through making them. They are a clue to the distinguishing differences and distinctions of his personal and cultural identity.

These are the criteria that served as the basis for the selection of all the examples of crafts that are included in this volume. While they represent a diversity of sources, they have a kinship in their personal and humanizing qualities. These are the qualities that typify the true spirit of the arts and can do so much to consummate the search for individuality in contemporary living.

Comb. Brazil, Caraja Indians. Reed, fiber and feathers; 7⅝". (Courtesy: The Museum of Primitive Art, New York.)

Appendix: Technical Reference

This technical reference is pertinent to both the assemblage and structuring of crafts. It includes factual information that is generally needed in craftmaking.

TOOLS, MATERIALS AND MEDIUMS FOR CUTTING AND FASTENING

Cutting Tools
Scissors, shears, knives, razor blades, saws, drills, files, chisels, gouges, punches.

Fastening Tools
Needles, staplers, eyelet and rivet setters, pliers, clamps, vises, hammers, mallets, screwdrivers, soldering irons and torches.

Fastening Materials and Mediums

Metal Fasteners for Flexible Materials. Pins, paper clips, staples, eyelets, grommets, rapid rivets, snap fasteners, buckles.

Metal Fasteners for Rigid Materials. Nails, tacks, screws, screw hooks, screw eyes, screw posts, nuts, bolts, washers.

Adhesive Mediums and Materials
Adhesives are made of sticky, glutinous substances obtained from animal, vegetable and synthetic sources. The following classification relates the source and characteristics of the various adhesive mediums to their suitability for different materials and uses.

Water-Soluble Pastes. The starchy substances obtained from corn, wheat and other plants are processed and mixed with water to make water-soluble pastes. These are usually available in small jars and are quick and easy to use for small projects of paper and cardboard. Wallpaper pastes come in powdered form and can be mixed with water as needed. These are better for large work such as portfolios because they dry slowly and allow time for application and handling. These are also preferable for all types of papier-mâché. (See Chapter 7.)

Water-Soluble Glues. The hard gelatin obtained by boiling the hides, hoofs and bones of animals is the chief source of water-soluble glues. These glues have more tenacity than pastes and become very hard and brittle when dry. Though water-soluble during application, they resist moisture once thoroughly dry. It is usually necessary to scrape or chip away dried glues to remove them. Glues are used chiefly for porous material such as cork or wood.

Waterproof Pastes and Glues. Milk derivatives, such as casein, and synthetic resins are the basis for the manufacture of new types of "white glues" and glue emulsions. These waterproof adhesives are replacing most other types of adhesives for all types of craftmaking. They can be used in a wide range of consistencies, from thin, liquid types to very thick, gelatinous types. They are very versatile for all types of materials; they can be used to adhere thin tissue papers as well as heavy woods. They can be diluted with water but are thoroughly waterproof when dry.

Plastic Cements. Synthetic resins are the base for plastic cements. Because they dry instantly, they are only suitable for joining small parts. They dry stiff and clear and are usually used for mending china or for model-making. They require quick handling because acetone and other acrylic solvents, which are used to liquefy the resins, evaporate so fast.

Epoxy Cements. Plastic resins are also used as the base for epoxy cements. They are prepared in two different mixtures; one of these is a hardening agent which must be combined with the other at the time of use. These are slow-drying and durable. They are particularly suitable for the adhesion of unlike materials such as metal to wood or plastic to metal.

Rubber Cements. Rubber cements are derived from natural or synthetic latex or gum resins that are characterized by elasticity. Benzol is the solvent, which evaporates immediately after the cement is applied. This adhesive has a number of unique features. It dries flat without warping; any excess smudges or smears can be rubbed off; if applied to only one of the surfaces to be joined, it can be used as a temporary binder; the material which is attached can be peeled off without damage. Since rubber cement is elastic, it is ideal for leather and other materials and products that require flexing.

Dry-Mounting Adhesive Materials. Plastic-coated sheets of paper are used as the base for dry-mounting adhesives. Adhesion takes place when heat and pressure are applied over a protective sheet of paper. An ordinary household electric iron can be used at low temperature for small work. However, a special dry-mounting press is needed for large work. The chief advantage of dry-mounting is that the results are neat, clean and flat. This type of material is used chiefly for mounting photographs and for flat items like place mats or portfolios.

Spray Adhesives. Plastic material similar to that used for masking tapes is the base for spray adhesives. They are quick and effective for binding papers and fabrics. It is easy to control and distribute the adhesive evenly. They dry flexible.

Adhesive Tapes. Either water-soluble or waterproof mediums can be used for the manufacture of adhesive tapes. The common gummed-paper tapes are coated with a water-soluble glue or mucilage. They require moistening and must be dried under pressure to prevent warping. The various masking tapes and self-adhering pressure tapes are coated with a plastic-base medium. They are quick to apply, but are chiefly used for temporary holds.

Adhesive Cloth. Plastic-base material which is subject to heat and pressure for adhesion is the base for all types of adhesive cloth. An ordinary electric iron is used to apply the cloth to other fabric, felt, leather, paper and many other flexible materials. The joining is permanent and very durable. The material can be washed or dry-cleaned.

BASIC DESIGN ARRANGEMENTS AND GROUPINGS

Symmetrical Balance

To achieve symmetrical balance, matching sizes, shapes, colors, and textures are placed on each side of center in corresponding positions.

Asymmetrical Balance

Unlike sizes, shapes, colors and textures can be used for asymmetrical balance. For example, several small pieces on one side of center can compensate for a single large shape on the other side. A small bit of brilliant color can be used to balance the attention that is attracted by a large shape of muted color on the opposite side.

It is necessary to equalize the visual interest from side to side and from different points of view.

Multiple Grouping

Regular Repetition. For groupings of regular repetition, the same kind of unit is placed in the same relative position over and over again.

Alternate Repetition. Two or more units of different sizes, shapes, colors or textures are combined in a sequence of changes for patterns of alternate repetition. Identical units can also be arranged in groupings of alternate repetition by changing the relative position above or below or from side to side.

Diminishing Sizes. Units of material in a range of different sizes can be grouped progressively from small to large to create patterns of diminishing sizes.

Dual Grouping. Identical sizes and shapes are used to make sets or pairs for dual grouping. Similar shapes and forms can be used for coordinated mispairment.

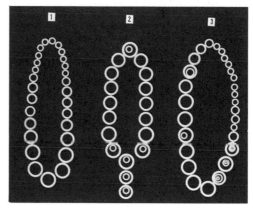

Multiple Grouping
(1) Symmetrical balance: diminishing sizes.
(2) Symmetrical balance: changes in size and placement of units for emphasis.
(3) Asymmetrical balance: changes in size, placement and kinds of units.

Multiple Grouping
(1) Regular repetition of identical units.
(2) Alternate repetition of identical units; changes in placement from side to side.
(3) Alternate repetition: changes in size.
(4) Alternate repetition: changes in size and number of units.
(5) Alternate repetition: changes in size, number and kinds of units.
(6) Alternate repetition: changes in size, number, units and placement.

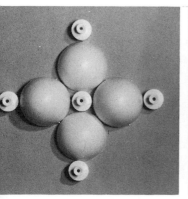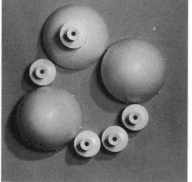

(Above, left) Symmetrical balance. Matching sizes and shapes of material are placed on each side of center.

(Above, right) Asymmetrical balance. Several of the smaller units are arranged on one side of center to compensate for the larger units on the other side.

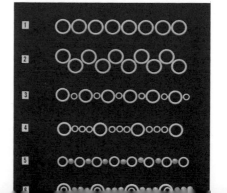

Some Sources for Crafts Materials

GENERAL ARTS AND CRAFTS SUPPLY COMPANIES

Allcraft Tool and Supply Company, Inc.; 22 West 48th St., New York, New York 10036

Bergen Arts and Crafts; Shetland Industrial Park, Salem, Massachusetts 01970

Arthur Brown and Brothers, Inc.; 2 West 46th St., New York, New York 10036

C C M Arts and Crafts, Inc.; 9520 Baltimore Ave., College Park, Maryland 20740

The Craftool Company; 1 Industrial Rd., Wood-Ridge, New Jersey 07075

Dennison Manufacturing Company; 300 Howard St., Framingham, Massachusetts 01701

The Handcrafters; 1 West Brown St., Waupun, Wisconsin 53963

Immerman Crafts, Inc.; 21668 Libby Rd., Cleveland, Ohio 44137

J. C. Larson; 7330 North Clark St., Chicago, Illinois 60626

Magnus Craft Materials; 109 Lafayette St., New York, New York 10013

Nasco—House of Crafts; Fort Atkinson, Wisconsin 53538

Sax Arts and Crafts; 207 North Milwaukee St., Milwaukee, Wisconsin 53202

Talens and Sons, Inc.; P.O. Box 453, Union, New Jersey 07083

Triarco Arts and Crafts; P.O. Box 106, Northfield, Illinois 60093

ADHESIVES AND FASTENERS

Borden, Inc., Chemical Division; 350 Madison Ave., New York, New York 10017

Bro-Dart Industries; 56 East St., Newark, New Jersey 07114

Growpac, Inc., (Pastemaker Division); 200 Broadhollow Rd., East Farmingdale, New York 11735

Le Page's, Inc.; 5850 Center Ave., Pittsburgh, Pennsylvania 15206

Mandus—Nelson Company; 564 West Adams St., Chicago, Illinois 60606

Minnesota Mining and Manufacturing Company; 6850 South Harlem Ave., Bedford Park, Illinois 60631

Sanford Ink Company; 2740 Washington Blvd., Bellwood, Illinois 60104

MEDIUMS: CHALKS, CRAYONS, INKS, PAINTS, PENCILS

American Crayon Company; 1706 Hayes Ave., Sandusky, Ohio 44870

Binney and Smith, Inc.; 380 Madison Ave., New York, New York 10017

Milton Bradley Company; 74 Park St., Springfield, Massachusetts 01101

Carter's Ink Company; 239 First St., Cambridge, Massachusetts 02142

The Craftint Manufacturing Company; 18501 Euclid Ave., Cleveland, Ohio 44112

Crayon, Water Color and Craft Institute; Eden Hill Rd., Newton, Connecticut 06470

Eagle Pencil Company; Eagle Rd., Danbury, Connecticut 06810

A. W. Faber—Castel—Higgins, Inc.; 41-47 Dickerson St., Newark, New Jersey 07103

Floquil Products, Inc.; Cobleskill, New York 12043

M. Grumbacher, Inc.; 460 West 34th St., New York, New York 10001

Higgins Ink Company, Inc.; 271 Ninth St., Brooklyn, New York 11215

Hunt Manufacturing Company; 1405 Locust St., Suite 1300, Philadelphia, Pennsylvania 19102

Kohinoor, Inc.; 100 North St., Bloomsbury, New Jersey 08804

Markal Company; 250 North Washtenaw Ave., Chicago, Illinois 60612

Naz-Dar Company; 1087 North Branch, Chicago, Illinois 60622

Pentel of America, Ltd.; 333 North Michigan Ave., Chicago, Illinois 60601

Permanent Pigments, Inc.; 2700 Highland Ave., Norwood, Ohio 45212

Rich Art Color, Inc.; 31 West 21st St., New York, New York 10010

Sanford Ink Company; 2740 Washington Blvd., Bellwood, Illinois 60104

Shiva Artist's Colors; 10th and Monroe St., Paducah, Kentucky 42001

Talens and Son; P.O. Box 453, Union, New Jersey 07083

Weber-Costello Company; 1900 North Narragansett Ave., Chicago, Illinois 60639

Winsor and Newton, Inc.; 555 Winsor Drive, Secaucus, New Jersey 07094

CORD AND ROPE

American Cotton Yarns, Inc.; 5825 South Western Ave., Chicago, Illinois 60621

Celanese Corporation of America; 180 Madison Ave., New York, New York 10016

Contessa Yarns; P.O. Box 37, Lebanon, Connecticut 06249

Hughes Fawcett, Inc., 115 Franklin St., New York, New York 10013

Lily Mills Company; Dept. HWSA, Shelby, North Carolina 28150

Midwest Cordage and Twine Specialties, Inc.; 3238 North Clark St., Chicago, Illinois 60657

National Cotton Council of America; P.O. Box 12285, Memphis, Tennessee 38101

P.C. Herwig Company; 268 Washington St., Brooklyn, New York 11201

Troy Yarn and Textile Company; 603 Mineral Springs Ave., Pawtucket, Rhode Island 02860

CORK

Chicago Cork Works Company; 6001 Gross Point Rd., Niles, Illinois 60648
Dodge Cork Company; 7300 South Central Ave., Bedford Park, Illinois 60638
Simmons and Associates—Decorative Cork; 5483 North N. W. Highway, Chicago, Illinois 60630
Sommer Cork Company, Inc.; 6342 West Irving Park Road, Chicago, Illinois 60634

FELT

G. A. F. Felt Products Corporation; 1950 Hawthorne, Melrose Park, Illinois 60160
Local department stores.

LEATHER: SKINS, HIDES, LACINGS, FASTENINGS, TOOLS

Avalon Industries, Inc.; 95 Lorimer St., Brooklyn, New York 11206
Crafts of Cleveland Leather Company; 2824 Lorain Ave., Cleveland, Ohio, 44113
Groton and Knight Company; Worcester, Massachusetts 01601
Herman Oak Leather Company; 4050 North First St., St. Louis, Missouri 63147
National Handicraft Company, Inc.; 225 Lafayette St., New York, New York 10012
Omega Leathercraft Products Company; Fort Worth, Texas 76101
Tandy Leather Company; P.O. Box 791, Fort Worth, Texas 76101. (Nationwide listings in local directories.)
Vanguard Crafts, Inc.; 2915 Avenue J., Brooklyn, New York 11236

METAL: SHEETS AND WIRE/TOOLS AND EQUIPMENT/FINDINGS

Allcraft Tool and Supply Company, Inc.; 215 Park Ave., Hicksville, New York 11801. (New York Salesroom: 22 W. 48 St., New York, New York 10036)
American Metalcraft, Inc.; 4100 West Belmont Ave., Chicago, Illinois 60641
Central States Roll Leaf Company; 2329 Hampton Ave., St. Louis, Missouri 63110
William Dixon, Inc.; 32 Kinney St., Newark, New Jersey 07102
Evans Findings Company, Inc.; 55 John St., Providence, Rhode Island 02904
Fellowcrafters, Inc.; 64 Stanhope St., Boston, Massachusetts 02109
Handy and Harman; 850 Third Ave., New York 10022
C. R. Hill Company (for metal foils); 35 West Grand River, Detroit, Michigan 48226
Ernest Linick and Company; 5 South Wabash Ave., Chicago, Illinois 60603

Riverside Alloy Metal Division: H. K. Porter, Inc.; 1021 Stuyvesant Ave., Union, New Jersey 07083
The Sculp-Metal Company; 701 Investment Bldg., Pittsburgh, Pennsylvania 15222

PAPERS AND CARDBOARDS

Aiko (Japanese imports); 714 North Wabash Ave., Chicago, Illinois 60611
Bemis-Jason Corporation (for tissue papers and special papers); 3250 Ash St., Palo Alto, California 94300
Pyramid Paper Company; 3530 West Fifth Ave., Chicago, Illinois 60624
Strathmore Paper Company; West Springfield, Massachusetts 01089

PLASTIC: MATERIAL AND TOOLS, CEMENTS AND FINDINGS

The Castolite Corporation (for liquid plastics for casting); Woodstock, Illinois 60098
Celanese Plastic Corporation; 180 Madison Ave., New York, New York 10016. Cadillac Plastics (local jobber for Celanese Corporation); 727 West Lake St., Chicago, Illinois 60606
Du Pont de Nemours Company, Inc.; Arlington, New Jersey 07032
Hollywood Plasties, Inc.; 4560 Worth St., Los Angeles, California 90063
Joli Plastics and Chemical Corporation; 1234 West 134 St., Gardena, California 90247
Rohm and Haas Company; 222 West Washington Square, Philadelphia, Pennsylvania 19105

RAFFIA AND REED

Bergen Arts and Crafts; Shetland Industrial Park, Salem, Massachusetts 01970
C C M Arts and Crafts, Inc.; 9520 Baltimore Ave., College Park, Maryland 20740
Creative Hands Company, Inc.; 4146 Library Rd., Pittsburgh, Pennsylvania 15234
Dick Blick Company; P.O. Box 1267, Galesburg, Illinois 61401
The Handcrafters; 1-99 West Brown St., Waupun, Wisconsin 53963

WOOD

Anco Wood Specialties, Inc.; 71-08 80th St., Glendale, New York 11227
Craftsman Wood Service Company (domestic and imported woods); 2727 Mary St., Chicago, Illinois 60608
U. S. Plywood Corporation; 103 Park Ave., New York, New York 10017
Local lumberyards

Bibliography

PART ONE LOOKING AT CRAFTS
Chapter 1, Introduction to Crafts

Battcock, Gregory, editor. *The New Art.* New York: Dutton, 1966.

Bayer, Herbert; Walter Gropius; and Ise Gropius, editors. *Bauhaus 1919–1928.* Boston: Branford, 1952.

Christensen, Erwin O. *Index of American Design.* New York: Macmillan, 1950.

Drexler, Arthur; and Greta Daniel. *Introduction to Twentieth-Century Design:* Collection of the Museum of Modern Art. New York: Doubleday, 1959.

Hughes, Graham. *Modern Silver throughout the World 1880–1967.* New York: Viking, 1967.

Manley, Seon. *Adventures in Making: The Romance of Crafts Around the World.* New York: Vanguard, 1959.

Mumford, Lewis. *Technics and Civilization.* New York: Harcourt, 1934.

Read, Herbert. *Art and Industry.* London: Faber and Faber, 1966.

Scheidig, Walther. *Crafts of the Weimar Bauhaus 1919–1924.* New York: Reinhold, 1967.

Slivka, Rose; Aileen O. Webb; and Margaret Merwin Patch. *The Crafts of the Modern World.* New York: Horizon Press in collaboration with The World Crafts Council, 1968.

Wallace, Don. *Shaping America's Products.* New York: Reinhold, 1956.

PART TWO CRAFTS OF ASSEMBLAGE
Chapters 2, 3, 4 and 5

Accorsi, William. *Toy Sculpture.* New York: Reinhold, 1968.

D'Amico, Victor; and Arlette Buchman. *Assemblage.* New York: The Museum of Modern Art, 1972.

Lord, Lois. *Collage and Construction in School.* Worcester, Massachusetts: Davis, 1960.

Rasmusen, Henry; and Art Grant. *Sculpture from Junk.* New York: Reinhold, 1967.

Reed, Carl; and Joseph Orze. *Art from Scrap.* Worcester, Massachusetts: Davis, 1960.

Seitz, William. *The Art of Assemblage.* New York: The Museum of Modern Art, 1961.

Simpson, Thomas. *Fantasy Furniture.* New York: Reinhold, 1968.

PART THREE CRAFTS OF STRUCTURED MATERIALS
Chapter 6, Basic Tools and Processes

Brady, George Stuart. *Materials Handbook.* New York: McGraw-Hill, 1963.

Brett, Guy. *Kinetic Art.* New York: Van Nostrand Reinhold, 1968.

Griswold, Lester and Kathleen. *The New Handicraft.* New York: Van Nostrand Reinhold, 1972.

Lynch, John. *How to Make Mobiles.* New York: Studio/Crowell, 1953.

Mayer, Ralph. *The Artist's Handbook of Materials and Techniques.* New York: Viking, 1970.

Willoughby, George A. *General Crafts.* Peoria, Illinois: Bennett, 1959.

Zechlin, Ruth. *Complete Book of Handicrafts.* Newton Center, Massachusetts: Branford, 1959.

Chapter 6, Design

Anderson, Donald. *Elements of Design.* New York: Holt, Rinehart, and Winston, 1961.

Ballinger, Louise Bowen; and Thomas F. Vroman. *Design Sources and Resources.* New York: Reinhold, 1965.

Brodatz, Phil. *Textures: A Photographic Album for Artists and Designers.* New York: Dover, 1966.

De Sausmarez, Maurice. *Basic Design: The Dynamics of Visual Form.* New York: Reinhold, 1964.

Guyler, Vivian Varney. *Design in Nature.* Worcester, Massachusetts: Davis, 1970.

Malcolm, Dorothea C. *Design: Elements and Principles.* Worcester, Massachusetts: Davis, 1972.

Mosely, Spencer; Pauline Johnson and Hazel Koenig. *Crafts Design.* Belmont, California: Wadsworth, 1962.

Proctor, Richard. *The Principles of Pattern for Craftsmen and Designers.* New York: Van Nostrand Reinhold, 1969.

Pye, David. *The Nature of Design.* New York: Reinhold, 1964.

Randall, Reino; and Edward C. Haines. *Design in Three Dimensions.* Worcester, Massachusetts: Davis, 1965.

Strache, Wolfe. *Forms and Patterns in Nature.* New York: Pantheon, 1956.

Chapter 7, Crafts of Flexible Materials: Felt and Leather

Enthoven, Jacqueline. *The Stitches of Creative Embroidery.* New York: Reinhold, 1964.

Guild, Vera P. *Creative Use of Stitches.* Worcester, Massachusetts: Davis, 1969.

Karasz, Mariska. *Adventures in Stitches.* New York: Funk and Wagnalls, 1959.

Krohn, Margaret B.; and Phyllis W. Schwebke. *How to Sew Leather, Suede, and Fur.* Milwaukee: Bruce, 1966.

Petersen, Grete; and Elsie Svennas. *Handbook of Stitches.* New York: Van Nostrand Reinhold, 1970.

Thompson, R. W. *How to Lace.* Los Angeles: E. V. Drake, 1952.

Waterer, John W. *Leather Craftsmanship.* New York: Praeger, 1968.

Willcox, Donald. *Modern Leather Design.* New York: Watson-Guptill, 1969.

Chapter 7, Crafts of Flexible Materials: Metal

Martin, Charles J.; and Victor D'Amico.

How to Make Modern Jewelry. New York: Simon and Schuster, 1949.

Stevens, R. W. *Simple Jewelry.* New York: Watson-Guptill, 1966.

Ullrich, Heinz; and Dieter Klante. *Creative Metal Design.* New York: Reinhold, 1968.

Von Neumann, Robert. *The Design and Creation of Jewelry.* New York: Chilton, 1967.

Weiner, Louis. *Handmade Jewelry.* New York: Van Nostrand, 1960.

Chapter 7, Crafts of Flexible Materials: Paper

Angrave, Bruce. *Sculpture in Paper.* New York: Crowell, 1957.

Betts, Victoria Bedford. *Exploring Papier-Mâché.* Worcester, Massachusetts: Davis, 1966.

Johnston, Mary Grace. *Paper Sculpture.* Worcester, Massachusetts: Davis, 1965.

Lipski, Tadeus. *Paper Sculpture.* New York: Crowell, 1948.

Rottger, Ernst. *Creative Paper Design.* New York: Reinhold, 1965.

Made with Paper. Catalog of Exhibition. New York: Museum of Contemporary Crafts, 1967.

Chapter 8, Crafts of Rigid Materials: Cork, Plastic and Wood

Aller, Doris. *Wood Carving Book.* Menlo Park, California: Lane, 1951.

Cherry, Raymond. *General Plastics.* Bloomington, Illinois: McKnight and McKnight, 1955.

Crowell, Thomas T. *Plexiglas Craftsman's Handbook.* Philadelphia: Rohm and Haas Co., 1954.

Meilach, Dona Z. *Contemporary Art with Wood.,* New York: Crown, 1968.

Newman, Thelma. *Plastics as an Art Form.* Philadelphia: Chilton, 1972.

Rottger, Ernst. *Creative Wood Design.* New York: Reinhold, 1963.

Chapter 9, Crafts of Linear Material: Cord and Rope, Raffia and Reed, Wire

Andes, Eugene. *Practical Macramé.* New York: Van Nostrand Reinhold, 1971.

Brommer, Gerald T. *Wire Sculpture and Other Three-Dimensional Construction.* Worcester, Massachusetts: Davis, 1968.

Christopher, F. J. *Basketry.* New York: Dover, 1952.

Hartung, Rolf. *Creative Textile Design—Thread and Fabric.* New York: Reinhold, 1965.

Harvey, Virginia I. *Macramé—The Art of Creative Knotting.* New York: Van Nostrand Reinhold, 1972.

Paque, Joan. *Visual Instructional Macramé.* Milwaukee: Joan and Henry Paque, 1971.

Seyd, Mary. *Designing with String.* New York: Watson-Guptill, 1969.

PART FOUR AN EVALUATIVE VIEW
Chapter 10, Toward Appreciation of Crafts

Bossert, Helmuth T. *Folk Art of Europe.* New York: Praeger, 1953.

————. *Folk Art of Primitive People.* New York: Praeger, 1955.

Christensen, Erwin O. *Primitive Art.* New York: Crown, 1955.

Dockstader, Frederick. *Indian Art in Middle America.* Pre-Columbian and Contemporary Arts and Crafts of Mexico, Central America, and the Caribbean. Greenwich, Connecticut: New York Graphic Society, 1964.

————. *Indian Art in South America.* Greenwich, Connecticut: New York Graphic Society, 1964.

Faulkner, Ray; and Edwin Ziegfeld. *Art Today.* New York: Holt, Rinehart, and Winston, 1969.

Gardi, Rene. *African Crafts and Craftsmen.* New York: Van Nostrand Reinhold, 1970.

Linton, Ralph; and Paul S. Wingert. *Arts of the South Seas.* The Museum of Modern Art. New York: Simon and Schuster, 1946.

Lipman, Jean. *American Folk Art in Wood, Metal, and Stone.* New York: Dover, 1972.

Mattil, Edward L. *Meaning in Crafts.* Englewood Cliffs, New Jersey: Prentice-Hall, 1971.

Miles, Charles. *Indian and Eskimo Artifacts of North America.* Chicago: Regnery, 1963.

Munsterberg, Hugo. *The Folk Arts of Japan.* Rutland, Vermont: Tuttle, 1958.

Schinneller, James A. *Art/Search and Self-Discovery.* Scranton, Pennsylvania: International Textbook Co., 1968.

MAGAZINES AND PERIODICALS ON CRAFTS AND DESIGN

Arts and Activities. The Teacher's Arts and Crafts Guide. 8150 North Central Park Avenue, Skokie, Illinois 60076.

Craft Horizons. American Crafts Council. 44 West 53rd Street, New York, New York 10019.

Design. The Magazine of Creative Art. Design Publishing Co., Columbus, Ohio.

Design Quarterly. Walker Art Center, 1710 Lyndale Avenue South, Minneapolis, Minnesota 55403.

Industrial Design. Whitney Publications, 18 East 50th Street, New York, New York 10022.

Interiors. Whitney Publications, 18 East 50th Street, New York, New York 10022.

School Arts. Davis Publications, 50 Portland Street, Worcester, Massachusetts 01608

Sunset Magazine, Lane Magazine and Book Co., Menlo Park, California 94025

Woman's Day, Fawcett Publications, Greenwich, Connecticut 06830.

Index